PRACTICAL ETHICS

PRACTICAL ETHICS

A Collection of Addresses and Essays

HENRY SIDGWICK

With an Introduction by
Sissela Bok

New York   *Oxford* • *Oxford University Press*   *1998*

Oxford University Press

Oxford   New York

Athens   Auckland   Bangkok   Bogota   Bombay   Buenos Aires
Calcutta   Cape Town   Dar es Salaam   Delhi   Florence   Hong Kong
Istanbul   Karachi   Kuala Lumpur   Madras   Madrid   Melbourne
Mexico City   Nairobi   Paris   Singapore   Taipei   Tokyo   Toronto   Warsaw

and associated companies in
Berlin   Ibadan

Originally published in 1898.

Foreword copyright © 1998 by Sissela Bok

Published by Oxford University Press, Inc.
198 Madison Avenue, New York, New York 10016

Oxford is a registered trademark of Oxford University Press

Library of Congress Cataloging-in-Publication Data
Sidgwick, Henry, 1838–1900.
Practical ethics : a collection of addresses
and essays / Henry Sidgwick ; with a foreword by Sissela Bok.
p.   cm. — (Practical and professional ethics series)
"Originally published in 1889"—T.p. verso.
At head of title: Association for Practical and
Professional Ethics.
Includes bibliographical references.
ISBN 0-19-511288-1
1. Ethics.   2. Conduct of life.   I. Title.   II. Series.
BJ1581.2.S494   1997
170—dc21   97-7574

3 5 7 9 8 6 4 2

Printed in the United States of America
on acid-free paper

INTRODUCTION

Sissela Bok

[We should] bring into a more clear and consistent form the broad and general agreement as to the particulars of morality which we find among moral persons, making explicit the general conceptions of the good and evil in human life, of the normal relation of a man to his fellows, which this agreement implies. We should do this not vaguely, but aiming cautiously at as much precision as the subject admits, not avoiding difficulties, but facing them, so as to get beyond the platitudes of copyright morality to results which may be really of use in the solution of practical questions; and yet not endeavouring to penetrate to ultimate principles, on which—as I have said—we can hardly hope to come to rational agreement in the present state of philosophical thought.

Henry Sidgwick, *Practical Ethics,* Chapter 1

Practical Ethics, the last book that Henry Sidgwick published before his death in 1900, contains the distillation of a lifetime of reflection on ethics and on what it would take for ethical debate to be "really of use in the solution of practical questions." This work deserves to count as a classic in the field of practical and professional ethics, bringing uncommon succinctness, wit, and cogency to many of the issues of ethics in private and in public life still debated a century later. In addition, its pages echo with Sidgwick's reflections on the philosophers he found most challenging. Among them are Socrates, Aristotle, Kant, Butler, Bentham, and Mill, sometimes mentioned by name, more often not. Like these thinkers, Sidgwick had, throughout his career, refused to isolate the study of ethics from that of politics, religion, economics, and the arts. He had explored the distinctions and linkages and mutual influences among these different fields in earlier works, such as his essays on literature and *The Elements of Politics* and *Political Economy*.[1]

Issued in 1898 as a collection of lectures given between 1888 and 1897, *Practical Ethics* allows a fuller perspective on these works. It also provides an indispensable complement to Sidgwick's major treatise on moral theory, *The Methods of Ethics*, first published when he was thirty-six years old and revised for successive editions throughout his life.[2] Sidgwick uses the same Aristotelian phrase to delimit the territory that each of these two books covers. In the preface to the first edition of *The Methods of Ethics*, he announces that

> though my treatment of the subject is, in a sense, more practical than that of many moralists, since I am occupied from first to last in considering how conclusions are to be rationally reached in the familiar matter of our common daily life and actual practice; still, my immediate object—to invert Aristotle's phrase—is not Practice but Knowledge. . . . I have desired to concentrate the reader's attention, from first to last, not on the practical results to which our methods lead, but on the methods themselves.[3]

Twenty-four years later, in *Practical Ethics*, Sidgwick reverses that focus. He declares that the central aim of discussions under that heading should be "in the Aristotelian sense, not knowledge but action" (p. 5). But although his focus in the first book is on knowledge and method, and, in the second, on action, both books inevitably concern their interaction. To approach Sidgwick's thinking through either of the two books alone gives but a partial understanding of its scope and of the sense of drama, sometimes despair, with which he explored the prospects for relating theory and practice.

In his own life, as in his writings, Sidgwick took for granted that moral reflection and practical moral choice ought to interact. To be practical, ethics had to bring both greater understanding of, and greater capacity for, what he termed "right living." Sidgwick's letters and journals convey the seriousness with which he took moral choice in his personal life, as well as the time and energy that he devoted to efforts to bring about institutional, social, and political reform. He engaged in many forms of social and philanthropic work and took lively part in the great debates of his time about the distribution of resources among social classes, about the duties of doctors, lawyers, public officials, and clergy, and about Britain's relations with Ireland, its colonial ventures in Africa, and its military policies.

As a fellow at Trinity College in Cambridge and later as Knightsbridge Professor of Moral Philosophy there, Sidgwick also devoted himself to liberalizing the academic curriculum and to other reforms. Influenced by John Stuart Mill's *The Subjection of Women,* he labored long and strenuously, against much opposition, for opening university studies to women and, once victorious, for granting them degrees. Joining with the economist Alfred Marshall and other Cambridge liberals, including his wife— the educator, lecturer, and author Eleanor Sidgwick—he struggled to establish what became Newnham College at Cambridge, of which Eleanor Sidgwick was appointed the Principal in 1892.[4] In 1882, the two also helped found the Society for Psychical Research, of which Henry was the first president and Eleanor the eighth.

Given its significance in relation to Sidgwick's life and writings as well as for the field of practical and professional ethics, it is the more striking that *Practical Ethics* is so rarely mentioned. One looks in vain for references to it in course syllabi, bibliographies, case books, textbooks and other materials either in practical (or applied) ethics or in moral philosophy more generally.[5] It is as if the book had vanished into thin air.[6]

One of the reasons for its disappearance from public view may be that it was barely mentioned in the 633-page *Henry Sidewick, A Memoir,* published after Sidgwick's death by his brother Arthur and his wife Eleanor, replete though this volume is with excerpts from Sidgwick's letters and diaries.[7] This omission may be due to the greater importance that Eleanor Sidgwick attached to their joint endeavors in the activities of the Society for Psychical Research, covered in the *Memoir* in assiduous detail. It was perhaps natural that Eleanor Sidgwick should stress this part of their joint work in a book about her late husband's life and work begun so shortly after his death. But for Henry Sidgwick as for her, the efforts to achieve clarity about psychical research also had a strong empirical component, itself connected with the possibility of practical ethics. If they could achieve contact with the dead, that would provide empirical confirmation of some form of afterlife. In turn, such evidence would lend more credence to claims about the possibility of a divine ordering of the universe that might provide firm foundations for human conduct, and for reconciling the moral conflict that Sidgwick saw between duty and self-interest. Without at least the possibility of such foundations, Sidgwick found it hard to counter the sense of inevitable failure to which he points in the concluding paragraph of the first edition of *The Methods of Ethics*:

> [T]he whole system of our beliefs as to the intrinsic reasonableness of conduct must fall, without a hypothesis unverifiable by experience reconciling the Individual with the Universal Reason, without a belief, in some form or other, that the moral order which we see imperfectly realized in this actual world, is yet actually perfect. If we reject this belief, we may perhaps still find in the non-moral universe an adequate object for the Speculative Reason, capable of being in some sense ultimately understood. But the Cosmos of Duty is thus really reduced to a Chaos: and the prolonged effort of the human intellect to frame a perfect ideal of rational conduct is seen to have been foredoomed to inevitable failure.[8]

A friend recounts how Sidgwick, shortly after having completed the manuscript for *The Methods of Ethics*, pointed to it and said, "I have long wished and intended to write a work on Ethics. Now it is written. I have adhered to a plan I laid out for myself; its first word was to be 'Ethics,' its last word 'Failure.'"[9] For the second edition of *The Methods of Ethics*, colleagues had persuaded Sigdwick to change that last word; but ending the book with "scepticism" rather than with "failure" was as far as he felt prepared to go. In a footnote near the end of the book, he adds that he cannot bring himself to postulate a Supreme Being for purposes of practical moral choice so long as he sees no grounds for belief in such a Being as "a speculative moral truth"; and he cannot even imagine such a state of mind "except as a momentary half-willful irrationality, committed in a violent access of philosophic despair."[10]

Such philosophic despair and such temptations to what he considered irrationality were not unknown to Sidgwick himself. In March 1887, he notes in his diary that acknowledging the failure of his efforts to obtain evidence of immortality "affects me not as a man but as a moralist."[11] And looking back to what he had written in 1874, to the effect that "without some datum beyond experience 'the Cosmos of duty is reduced to a

Chaos,'" he asks what he has left to teach, having found no such datum. Should he recant his conviction and answer his own arguments?

> Or am I to use my position—and draw my salary—for teaching that Morality *is* a Chaos, from the point of view of Practical Reason; adding cheerfully that, as man is not after all a rational being, there is no real fear that morality won't be kept up somehow.[12]

The essays collected in *Practical Ethics,* offered first as public lectures starting the following year, must be read in the light of these doubts. Could there be an approach to ethics that did not call for examining its methods or foundations? Could there be methods of constructing some form of Moral Cosmos short of one ordained and supported by a Supreme Being? Could there be ways of debating practical moral choice that would not call for framing "a perfect ideal for rational conduct" as a preliminary?

To explore these questions, Sidgwick chose a new approach. He reached beyond the academy to discuss them with men and women from different professional, educational, and religious backgrounds in the Cambridge Ethical Society that he had helped to found. The Cambridge society was modeled in part, as were the ethical societies founded a few years later in London, on the Societies for Ethical Culture recently inaugurated in America.[13] Members of these societies were to meet periodically for purpose of "promoting, through intelligent discussion the interests of practical morality."[14] Together, members might consider such questions as when, if ever, public officials might be justified in lying or in breaking promises, whether scientists could legitimately inflict suffering on animals for research purposes, and when nations might have just cause in going to war. In this way, they might reasonably strive to reach "some results of value for practical guidance and life."[15]

Most of the essays in the present volume were first presented as addresses to one or another of these societies. In the first essay, "The Scope and Limits of the Work of an Ethical Society," Sidgwick warns his audience about the reasons so many debates about practical ethics founder in disputes about vast unresolved theoretical issues. The likelihood of failure is strong, he suggests. He offers, as a cautionary example, the fate of a metaphysical society in London to which he had belonged. Its members had come together with high hopes to debate profound topics such as the meaning of human life, the relation of the finite to the infinite, the ultimate ground of duty, or the essence of virtue; but after much convivial discussion, it had become clear that no joint progress had been made with respect to these topics. No one had convinced anyone else and "we all remained exactly as we were."

If members of the society hoped to fare better and to reach results of practical value, they "should give up altogether the idea of getting to the bottom of things, arriving at agreement on the first principles of duty or the Summum Bonum."[16] To prevent them from slipping into their accustomed debates over imponderables, Sidgwick urges them to remain, as much as possible, in what he calls the "region of middle axioms."[17]

> Moralists of all schools have acknowledged . . . that broad agreement in the details of morality which we actually find both among thoughtful persons who profoundly disagree on first principles, and among plain men who do not seriously trouble themselves about first principles. Well, my view is that we ought to start with this broad agreement as to the dictates of duty, and keeping close to it, without trying to penetrate to the ultimate grounds. . . . We must remain as far as possible in the "region of middle axioms," if I may be permitted the technical term.[18]

The term "middle axioms" was one Sidgwick had adopted from John Stuart Mill, who distinguished "axiomata media" or intermediate principles, "on the one hand, from empirical laws resulting from simple observation and, on the other from the highest generalizations."[19] Mill, in turn, had referred to Francis Bacon, who wrote in *Novum Organon* of the understanding proceeding "by a true scale and successive steps, without interruption or breach, from particulars to the lesser axioms, thence to the intermediate (rising one above the other), and lastly, to the most general."[20] Sidgwick suggests to his audience that the region of middle axioms might provide a common moral ground for their debates, even though they do not share the most general moral principles or metaphysical premises. This common ground should be explored with "as much precision as the subject admits, not avoiding difficulties, but facing them, so as to get beyond the platitudes of copybook morality to results which may be really of use in the solution of practical questions."[21]

What might debates be like that remained in such a region of middle axioms? First, participants must agree not to take up perennially disputed metaphysical questions such as those Sidgwick had mentioned in connection with the Metaphysical Society, including inquiries into the most general foundations of morality; but to acknowledge, rather, "the broad and general agreement as to particulars of morality which we find among moral persons" (p. 7). Sidgwick offers as such particulars the principles of *veracity, justice,* and *good faith,* or fidelity to promises. Unlike the most general principles of morality, these particulars, or middle principles, allow for exceptions, which can be usefully discussed in the context of different sorts of examples. Such a discussion, which must involve efforts at line-drawing, might well be characterized as one of "casuistry"—an undertaking he adds, that has been poorly understood and therefore too hastily set aside.[22] Instead, members of the society should press for greater clarity in discussing particular cases and practices, work to dispel confusion, and reject spurious reasons for disagreement.

Second, the middle region is one in which the concern must be neither with strictly religious debates nor with strictly secular ones insofar as they would exclude the spiritual concerns that often have religious roots. There need be no references to the supernatural nor to a future life, Sidgwick suggests, as providing rewards for virtuous conduct. Rather, there could be broad agreement on a large overlapping region of secular duty that is found, in fact, also in religious contexts and that can be shared quite independently of revelation. The work of the Ethical Society should, Sidewick insisted, be confined to this shared secular middle region, which need in no way therefore be irreligious, nor be used to exclude participants from any one religious background.[23]

Third, Sidgwick proposes that discussions within the region of middle axioms should leave aside topics that require a "detailed study of social facts."[24] Not that such facts should be excluded, he adds, but the main focus of the society should be on mid-level practical principles and on their practical application. So, for example, instead of considering particular moral choices for a lawyer or a public servant, members might take up possible exceptions to common moral ideals that professionals advocate for their own group. For instance, all would agree that it is prima facie wrong for them to lie or to break promises. But when, if at all, might lawyers nevertheless legitimately urge false or misleading considerations for their clients? Or a government repudiate an international treaty?

A note appended at the end of the first essay bespeaks the difficulties of remaining within the limits that Sidgwick had proposed to the Cambridge Ethical Society. They had been found "too narrow by the leading spirits of the London Ethical Society." But Sidgwick would not give up without a struggle. In 1893, when he gave his presidential address to the latter group—the second essay in this book—it had been in existence for several years; and it ran the risk, so one senses in his essay, of going the way of the metaphysical society—of losing itself in congenial but ineffectual exchanges on the "ultimate grounds."

This second essay has to be read as a profoundly personal declaration on Sidgwick's part, suggesting how he thought the London Ethical Society might be able to right its course without abandoning its larger aspirations. Sidgwick has given anxious thought, he admits, to what his duty as president might be: if he is honest in delineating the difficulties facing any group having set for itself the goals of the present society, will he not repel some members from the study it aims to promote? Yet the duty of his position as the society's president is clear. He has to help members see the seriousness of the obstacles they confront in reconciling their declared aims on the basis of their declared principles.

The society's members had stated as their goal not only the practical aim appropriate for such a group, "to assist in individual and social efforts after right living" (p. 16), but also one that might lead them far afield and at times conflict with the first: "to free the current ideal of what is right from all that is merely traditional and self-contradictory, and thus to widen and perfect it" (p. 19). Still further from strictly practical purposes, they aimed "to assist in constructing as Theory or Science of Right, which, starting with the reality and validity of moral distinctions, shall explain their mental and social origin, and connect them in a logical system of thought" (p. 19).

It is no wonder that the effort to assist in constructing such a theory should give Sidgwick pause. Thinkers have endeavored to do so since time immemorial, and he himself had spent much of his life working for the same end. But practical ethics, if it is to "assist in individual and social efforts after right living," must proceed from a basis of more general agreement than can be had on the theoretical questions the group seeks to answer. Why not address even the theoretical questions from the middle ground of principles that can be shared by most persons? There is much more agreement on what a good life is, he points out, than on why it is good or on what its ultimate ends might be. Circumstances will inevitably change as will understandings of obligations relating to gender, family, and social class. But life, he concludes, "is essentially change, and the good life must be essentially life; it is enough if it contain unchanged amid the change that aspiration after the best life which is itself a chief source and spring of change" (p. 30).

What role should philosophers play in the process of elucidating both theory and practice when it comes to such a good life? Sidgwick explains why they neither can nor ought to undertake such an inquiry alone. The reasons he gives are hard won, though he thought earlier that philosophers had a more central role than he now believes fruitful. One detects none of the youthful arrogance of his *Methods of Ethics*, with its distinctions between "the enlightened few" and "the vulgar," and its endorsement of special moral exemptions for "a class of persons defined by exceptional qualities of intellect, temperament, and character."[25] Instead, Sidgwick sets forth mutual advantages for philosophers and non-philosophers in making common cause in its service. While the discussion of ethical issues can benefit from the clarification and analysis that philosophers bring, they need, in turn, to draw on the knowledge of facts and the experience of persons "in the thick and heat of the struggle of active life, in all stations and ranks, in the churches and outside the churches" (p. 22).

The third and fourth essays of the book, entitled "Public Morality," and "The Morality of Strife," are of great interest for contemporary discussions of public and private ethics and of the morality of war and peace.[26] Is there a distinction, Sidgwick asks in "Public Morality," between public and private morality? It would surely be a deep paradox, he argues, if lawyers and doctors and other professionals saw fit to override the most common moral precepts of justice, veracity, and good faith when it suited them, and that of "abstinence from aggression on person or property" that he sometimes cites as belonging to the same set of basic precepts. But whereas most might agree about how these principles should hold for most professionals, the same is not the case when it comes to government morality. Clearly, public officials are not holding themselves to such rules in practice. Sometimes their justification for breaches are "esoteric"—not defended publicly. But, increasingly, Sidgwick adds, one encounters open defenses of government aggression or bad faith reminiscent of Machiavelli.

He considers the nineteenth-century advocates of Machiavellian views and points out that, as a utilitarian, it is not the view that the ends justify the means to which he objects, but such claims when they are made on the part of regional or sectarian rather than common human ends. A violation of rules of mutual behavior, he concludes, "so far as it is merely justified by its conduciveness to the sectional interest of a particular group of human beings, must receive unhesitating and unsparing censure" (p. 46).

In "The Morality of Strife," Sidgwick presses these issues in the context of war—the form of strife which "causes the most intense and profound moral aversion and perplexity to the modern mind" (p. 49). He considers reasons for going to war, compares views regarding just wars, alternative ways of resolving conflict such as arbitration, in ways that take on new meaning in the light of the century of warfare since his book appeared. Some of his observations resonate with understandable inability to foresee the wars and genocides that our own century would bring, as well as ignorance of massive human rights abuses perpetrated, even as he wrote, at home and abroad. As a result, Sidgwick could maintain that there was steady improvement in "a spirit of humanity"; and that, "considering the aims of war, and the deadly violence inevitable in its methods, I think that civilized humanity, at the end of the nineteenth century, may look with some complacency on the solid amount of improvement achieved" (p. 58).

The same hopefulness about the future is evident in the eighth essay, "The Pursuit of Culture," a lecture delivered in 1897. Sidewick opens by stressing the new role for practical ethics at the close of a century during which the sciences have brought unparalleled enlargement of "our conception of the prospective greatness of human life to be lived on this earth."[27] No more remarkable change has ever taken place in human thought: the life of the human race "now spreads out before our imagination as all but infinite in its probably duration and its possibilities of development" (p. 114). As a consequence, the problem of how to make human life on earth better has become the dominant problem for morality; a task which will be facilitated, Sidgwick declares, by the rejection of narrow individualism and "the enlarged conception of social and political duty which is now prevalent."

A century after Sidgwick's lecture, the survival of the human race has itself been placed in question, along with that of innumerable other species. If Sidgwick could have foreseen the technological and ideological developments that have brought about these risks, not perceived at his time, he might well insist that this only makes it more important to focus on what he saw as the "dominant problem for morality," only to do so in awareness of all the ways in which simplistic efforts to do so can go astray.

Contemporary readers may find it odd, even disproportionate, that Sidgwick should devote two of his nine essays in a volume entitled *Practical Ethics* to the moral issues raised by temptations to hypocrisy and deceit among the clergy. In "The Ethics of Religious Conformity" and "Clerical Veracity," Sidgwick returns to discuss the question of veracity that he had already considered in "Public Morality" and earlier in *The Methods of Ethics*—but with focus this time on the clergy. Might they have special reasons to engage in "pious fraud," for the sake of the greater good that they might thereby be able to bring about in their congregations? Sidgwick takes up, in this context, conflicts within the Church of England about whether it could be permissible for a clergyman to profess every Sunday a belief in the Apostle's Creed that he did not in fact entertain; he concludes that on both moral and religious grounds, actual falsehoods must be ruled out.

In examining what he took to be the hypocrisy surrounding such declarations, and concluding that they represented a serious form of deceit, Sidgwick could draw on personal experience in the late 1860s. As a young fellow and assistant tutor at Trinity, he had gradually gone from orthodoxy with respect to Church of England teachings to increasingly greater religious doubts. He had finally concluded that he could not subscribe to some of the dogmas embodied in the articles of the Apostle's Creed that academics were enjoined to affirm each year. He could ill afford to lose his academic position, however, and knew that by refusing the religious test he would distress many in his family, especially his mother. Finally, he chose to speak out and to submit a proposal to abolish religious tests for fellows. These tests, which included profession of belief in the Apostle's Creed, made it impossible for agnostics, dissenters, Catholics, and others to hold fellowships. The proposal was turned down, and Sidgwick resigned his fellowship in June 1868. Other Trinity Fellows followed his example. Trinity, however, rehired him as a lecturer and abolished the religious tests altogether the next year. In 1871, they were eliminated at all universities by an Act of Parliament.[28] A historian of the period comments on Sidgwick's choice: "It was the purely voluntary act of a high-minded and very scrupulous man who thought no sacrifice too great on behalf of honesty. It is impossible to exaggerate the moral splendor of his action."[29]

Given Sidgwick's own willingness to take great risks for the sake of personal honesty and his stance with respect to "pious fraud," it is the more striking that he should be considerably more cavalier with respect to lies by persons in other walks of life—by doctors to their patients or by homeowners to burglars, or by spies and police agents. In *The Methods of Ethics,* likewise, he had jumbled together untruths "told to children, or madmen, or invalids, or by advocates or to enemies or robbers" as not clearly wrong in the eyes of Common Sense, based on unspecified "utilitarian reasonings."[30] The reasons he offers in *Practical Ethics* are still utilitarian, still uncharacteristically hasty and unclear, with no convincing explanation why some lies should be accepted on utilitarian grounds and not lies by the clergy.

Throughout these two essays, as in the others, Sidgwick nevertheless proceeds with a calm reasonableness and quick wit that invite further debate and reflection. Just as his manner of sorting out moral problems is known to have had that effect among his contemporaries, so it can contribute to our own debates about the many questions of practical ethics that he took up and the numerous new issues that have arisen since.

Were he to take part in tody's debates, he would doubtless pay special attention to the vast scale, both of opportunities and of problems, that the century since he published his book has brought to light. He might well wish to reiterate his belief, stated in "The Pursuit of Culture," that the problem of how to make human life on earth better has become the dominant one for morality, even as he might express greater doubts about his earlier confidence in the prevalence of an enlarged conception of social and political duty, especially in the light of the developments he did not foresee: the extraordinary growth in our century of the world's population, especially in the poorest societies; the humanly inflicted threats to the Earth's environment; and the unprecedented risks posed by the proliferation of nuclear weapons and other means of mass destruction.

As we consider these problems, along with the many ethical issues in personal and public life that confront individuals and societies today as they did in his time, we have much to gain by exploring the shared moral precepts that he considered central, and by using them as common ground within "the region of middle axioms" from which to launch further debates. We can benefit, too, from drawing on Sidgwick's clear-headed, searching approach to moral inquiry, both practical and theoretical. It was summed up, after his death, by one who knew him well: "He offered the highest type of a seeker after truth, more anxious to understand an opponent's argument than to refute him; watchful lest any element in a discussion should be left unnoticed; patient, reverent, ready to the last to welcome light from any quarter."[31]

Notes

1. Henry Sidgwick, *The Principles of Political Economy* (London: Macmillan & Co, 1883); *The Elements of Politics* (London: Macmillan & Co, 1891); for a complete bibliography, see Jerome Schneewind, *Sidgwick's Ethics and Victorian Moral Philosophy* (Oxford: Oxford University Press, 1977).

2. Henry Sidgwick, *The Methods of Ethics,* 1st ed. (London: Macmillan & Co, 1874). For an excellent treatment of this work in its historical context, see Jerome B. Schneewind, *Sidgwick's Ethics and Victorian Moral Philosophy* (Oxford University Press, 1977).

3. *Ibid,* Preface, p. vi.

4. Among works authored by Eleanor Sidgwick are "On the electrochemical equivalent of silver," co-authored with John S. Rayleigh (London: Philosophical Transactions of the Royal Society, 1884); *Health Statistics of Women Students of Cambridge and Oxford and of their sisters* (Cambridge University Press, 1890); *University Education of Women* (Cambridge: Macmillan and Bowes, 1897). Eleanor Sidgwick also edited *Henry Sidgwick: A Memoir,* with Arthur Sidgwick (London: Macmillan, 1906); *The International Crisis in Its Ethical and Psychological Aspects* (London: H. Milford, 1915); and *Phantasms of the Living* (London: K. Paul, Trench, Trubner & Co., 1918).

5. Even books with the very same title of *Practical Ethics,* published after Sidgwick's, do not refer to it. See the works with this title by Herbert Samuels (London: T. Butterworth Ltd., 1935); Peter Singer (Cambridge University Press, 1979; 2nd ed., 1993); Gordon Shea (New York: American Management Association Publications, 1988).

6. *Practical Ethics* was reissued once in 1909. The book is not mentioned at all in the issue of *The Monist* devoted to Sidgwick (Vol. 58, 1974). It is mentioned in a note to the Introduction in Bart Schultz, ed., *Essays on Henry Sidgwick* (Cambridge: Cambridge University Press, 1992); and in the bibliography of Sidgwick's works in Schneewind, *Sidgwick's Ethics.*

7. Apart from a few footnotes, the authors mention the book only once in the

text to indicate that Sidgwick had sent a copy to Bishop Creighton. They quote a passage from Creighton's letter concerning the book, and Sidgwick's letter in response, pp. 569–70.

8. Henry Sidgwick, *Methods of Ethics,* 1st ed., pp. 472–73. Quoted in Frank Miller Turner, *Between Science and Religion: The Reaction to Scientific Naturalism in Late Victorian England* (New Haven: Yale University Press, 1974), p. 47.

9. F. H. Hayward, quoting Oscar Browning, cited in Bart Schultz, "Introduction," in Schultz, ed., *Essays on Henry Sidgwick,* p. 4.

10. Sidgwick, *Methods of Ethics,* p. 507.

11. Henry Sidgwick, diary, March 16, 1887, in *Henry Sidgwick; A Memoir,* pp. 471–72. Earlier, on January 28, 1887, Sidgwick mentions that when he wrote his *Methods of Ethics,* he had been "inclined to hold, with Kant, that we must *postulate* the continued existence of the soul in order to effect that harmony of duty with Happiness which seemed to me indispensable to rational moral life." If now he decides the search is a failure, can he still make such a postulate? And if not, "have I any ethical system at all?" (p. 467).

12. *Ibid,* p. 472.

13. See I. D. MacKillop, *The British Ethical Societies* (Cambridge University Press, 1986); and G. Spiller, *The Ethical Movement in Great Britain* (London: printed for the author at the Farleigh Press, 1934).

14. *Practical Ethics,* p. 1.

15. The Societies included scientists, doctors, lawyers, theologians, and public officials. Among those present at some of these meetings may have been Eleanor Sidgwick, her brother Arthur Balfour, G. E. Moore and John Maynard Keynes, all three of whom had studied with Sidgwick, his scientist colleagues from Trinity College, A. Bain, the psychologist, and his wife named only "Mrs. Bain" in the issue of *Mind* (vol. 5, 1896, pp. 327–42) where she is the author of a critique of Sidgwick, entitled "Ethics From a Purely Practical Standpoint."

16. *Practical Ethics,* p. 5.

17. *Ibid,* p. 7.

18. *Ibid,* pp. 6, 7.

19. John Stuart Mill, *A System of Logic Ratiocinative and Inductive,* 1845 (London, Longmans, Green & Co., 1925), p. 568. In his essay "Bentham," Mill writes: "As mankind are much more nearly of one nature, than of one opinion about their own nature, they are more easily brought to agree in their intermediate principles—*vera illa et media axiomata,* as Bacon says—than in their first principles" ("Bentham" in Marshall Cohen, ed., *The Philosophy of John Stuart Mill,* New York: Modern Library, p. 47).

20. Francis Bacon, *Novum Organon,* I, 104.

21. Sidgwick, *Practical Ethics,* p. 7.

22. *Ibid,* pp. 11.

23. *Ibid,* p. 9.

24. *Ibid,* p. 11.

25. Sidgwick, *Methods of Ethics,* pp. 490, 489.

26. These essays were reprinted in 1918 in a volume edited by Viscount James Bryce under the title *National and International Right and Wrong: Two Essays.*

27. Sidgwick, *Practical Ethics,* p. 113.

28. See the accounts in Sidgwick and Sidgwick, *Henry Sidgwick,* Ch. III, Schneewind, *Sidgwick's Ethics,* pp. 21–40, and in Q. D. Leavis, "Henry Sidgwick's Cambridge," *Scrutiny,* Vol. XV, No 1, December 1947, pp. 2–11.

29. D. A. Winstanley, *Later Victorian Cambridge* (Cambridge: Cambridge University Press, 1947).

30. Sidgwick, *The Methods of Ethics,* p. 355.

31. Dr. Westcott, Bishop of Durham, Dec. 1900, quoted in A. and E. Sidgwick, *Henry Sidgwick, A Memoir,* p. 559.

PREFACE

THE greater part of the present volume consists of addresses delivered before one or other of the Ethical Societies that were founded some ten years ago in London and Cambridge. These societies were partly— though not entirely—modelled on the "Societies for Ethical Culture" which had been started in America a few years before: they aimed at meeting a need which was believed to be widely felt for the intelligent study of moral questions with a view to elevate and purify social life. At the first meeting of the Cambridge Ethical Society, in May, 1888, I endeavoured, in an address which I have placed first in this volume, to set forth my conception of the work that the Society might profitably undertake. Four years later, at a meeting of the London Ethical Society, of which I was at the time President, I attempted a somewhat fuller analysis of the aims and methods of such an association. This stands second in the volume. In three other addresses, delivered before one or other of these societies, I endeavoured to apply my general conception to particular topics of interest and difficulty—the "Morality of Strife," the "Ethics of Conformity," and "Luxury." These stand respectively fourth, fifth, and seventh in the volume. These addresses, except the first, have already appeared in the *International Journal of Ethics.*

Along with these addresses I have included four papers, having, either in whole or in part, similarly practical aims. Two of these, on "Public Morality" and "Clerical Veracity," and part of a third, on the "Pursuit of Culture," are published here for the first time. I have placed each of the three either before or after the address that appeared most cognate in subject. The connection is closest in the case of the paper on "Clerical Veracity"; which is, in fact, a fuller exposition—called forth by controversy—of my views on a portion of the subject of the address that precedes it. The last paper in the volume—on "Unreasonable Action"—I have not included without some hesitation, as it was written primarily from a psychological rather than a practical point of view: but on the whole it appeared to me to have sufficient ethical interest to justify its inclusion.

Newnham College, Cambridge   HENRY SIDGWICK
November 1897

CONTENTS

PRACTICAL ETHICS

would not necessarily be an evil at all. Even supposing that we become convinced in the course of two or three years that we are not going to attain the end that we have in view by the method which we now propose to use, we might still feel—I have good hope that we shall feel—that our discussions, so far as they will have gone, will have been interesting and, in their way, profitable; though recognizing that the time has come for the Ethical Society to cease, we may still feel glad that it has existed, and that we have belonged to it.

This cheerfully pessimistic view—if I may so describe it—is partly founded on an experience which I will briefly narrate.

Many years ago I became a member of a Metaphysical Society in London; that was its name, although it dealt with ethical questions no less than those called metaphysical in a narrow sense. It included many recognized representatives of different schools of thought, who met animated, I am sure, by a sincere desire to pursue truth by the method of discussion; and sought by frank explanation of their diverse positions and frank statement of mutual objections, to come, if possible, to some residuum of agreement on the great questions that concern man as a rational being—the meaning of human life, the relation of the individual to the universe, of the finite to the infinite, the ultimate ground of duty and essence of virtue. Well, for a little while the Society seemed to flourish amazingly; it was joined by men eminent in various departments of practical life—statesmen, lawyers, journalists, bishops and archbishops of the Anglican and of the Roman persuasion: and the discussions went on, monthly or thereabouts, among the members of this heterogeneous group, without any friction or awkwardness, in the most frank and amicable way. The social result was all that could be desired; but in a few years' time it became, I think, clear to all of us that the intellectual end which the Society had proposed to itself was not likely to be attained; that, speaking broadly, we all remained exactly where we were, "Affirming each his own philosophy," and no one being in the least convinced by any one else's arguments. And some of us felt that if the discussions went on, the reiterated statement of divergent opinions, the reiterated ineffective appeals to a common reason which we all assumed to exist, but which nowhere seemed to emerge into actuality, might become wearisome and wasteful of time. Thus the Metaphysical Society came to an end; but we were glad—at least, I certainly was glad—that we had belonged to it. We had not been convinced by each other, but we had learnt to understand each other better, and to sympathize, in a certain sense, with opposing lines of thought, even though we were unable to follow them with assent.

I have not, however, brought in this comparison merely to show why I am not afraid of failure; I have brought it in partly to introduce one counsel that I shall give to the Ethical Society with the view of escaping failure, viz., that it should be as much as possible *unlike* in its aims to the Metaphysical Society to which I have referred. I think we should give up altogether the idea of getting to the bottom of things, arriving at agreement on the first principles of duty or the Summum Bonum. If our discussions persist in taking that line, I can hardly doubt that we shall imitate the example of failure that I have just set before you; we shall not convince each other, and after a little while each of us, like the Irish juryman, will get tired of arguing with so many other obstinately unreasonable persons. In the Metaphysical Society we could not avoid this; a metaphysician who does not try to get to the bottom of things is, as Kant would say, an "Unding": he has no *raison d'être*. But with our Ethical Society the case is different; the aim of such an Ethical Society, in the Aristotelian phrase, is not knowledge but action: and with this practical object it is not equally necessary that we should get to the bottom of things. It would be presumptuous to suppose that in such a Society as this, including, as we hope, many members whose intellectual habits as well as their aims are practical rather than speculative, we can settle the old controversies of the schools on ethical first principles; but it may be possible by steering clear of these controversies to reach some results of value for practical guidance and life. But how exactly are we to do this?

The question may be put in a more general form, in which it has a wider and more permanent interest than we can presume to claim for the special purpose for which we are met here tonight. What, we may ask, are the proper lines and limits of ethical discussion, having a distinctly practical aim, and carried on among a miscellaneous group of educated persons, who do not belong exclusively to any one religious sect or philosophical school, and possibly may not have gone through any systematic study of philosophy? The answer that I am about to give to this question must not be taken as in any way official, nor do I intend it to be in any way cut and dried. I should like to be free to adopt a materially different view as the result of further experience and interchange of opinions. But at present the matter presents itself to me in this light. Moralists of all schools have acknowledged—and usually emphasized, each from his own point of view—that broad agreement in the details of morality which we actually find both among thoughtful persons who profoundly disagree on first principles, and among plain men who do not seriously trouble themselves about first principles. Well, my view is that we ought to start with this broad agreement as to the dictates of duty, and keeping close to it, without trying to penetrate to the ultimate grounds, the first principles on which duty may be constructed as a rational system, to make this general agreement somewhat more explicit and clear than it is in ordinary thought. I want to advance one or two degrees in the direction of systematizing morality without hoping or attempting to go the whole way; and in the clearer apprehension of our common morality thus gained to eliminate or reduce the elements of confusion, of practical doubt and disagreement, which, at the present day at least, are liable to perplex even the plainest of plain men. I sometimes wonder whether the great Bishop Butler, who lays so much emphasis on the clearness and certainty of the dictates of a plain man's conscience,—I wonder whether this generally cautious thinker would use quite the same language if he lived now. It certainly seems to me that the practical perplexities of the plain man have materially increased in the century and a half that have elapsed since the famous sermons to which I refer were preached. Take, e.g., the case of compassion. The plain man of Butler's time knew that when he heard the cry of distress he ought to put his hand in his pocket and relieve it; but now he has learnt from newspapers and magazines that indiscriminate almsgiving aggravates in the long run the evils that it attempts to cure; and, therefore now, when he hears the cry of woe, it is apt to stir in his mind a disagreeable doubt and conflict, instead of the old simple impulse. Well, there is a solution to this perplexity, on which thinkers of the most different schools and sects would probably agree: that true charity demands of us money, but also something more than money: personal service, sacrifice of time and thought, and—after all—a patient endurance of a partially unsatisfactory result, acquiescence in minimizing evils that we cannot cure.

But this answer, though it does not raise any of the fundamental questions disputed in the schools, is yet not altogether trite and obvious; to give it in a fully satisfactory form needs careful thinking over, careful development and explanation. Thus this case may serve to illustrate my view of the general function of ethical debate, carried on by such a society as ours: to bring into a more clear and consistent form the broad and general agreement as to the particulars of morality which we find among moral persons, making explicit the general conceptions of the good and evil in human life, of the normal relation of a man to his fellows, which this agreement implies. We should do this not vaguely, but aiming cautiously at as much precision as the subject admits, not avoiding difficulties, but facing them, so as to get beyond the platitudes of copybook morality to results which may be really of use in the solution of practical questions; and yet not endeavouring to penetrate to ultimate principles, on which—as I have said—we can hardly hope to come to rational agreement in the present state of philosophical thought. We must remain as far as possible in the "region of middle axioms"—if I may be allowed the technical term.

But how shall we mark off this region of discussion, in which we look for middle axioms, from the region in which first principles are sought? Well, I shall not try to do this with any definiteness, for if I did I should inevitably pass over into the region that I am trying to avoid; I should illustrate the old Greek argument to prove the necessity of philosophizing. "We must philosophize, for either we ought to philosophize, or, if we ought not, we must philosophize in order to demonstrate that we ought not to philosophize." So if I tried to make definite our general conception of the kind of topics we ought to avoid, I should be insensibly drawn into a full discussion of these topics. I shall, therefore, leave the line vague, and content myself with describing some of the questions that lie beyond it.

To begin, there is all the discussion as to the nature, origin and development of moral ideas and sentiments, which—in recent times especially—has absorbed so large a part of the attention of moralists; when we want them to tell us what morality is, they are apt to slide off into entertaining but irrelevant speculations as to how, in pre-historic times, or in the obscurity of the infant's consciousness, it came to be. I think that, for our present purposes, we must keep clear of all this; we must say, with the German poet, "Wir, wir leben . . . und der lebende hat Recht." We must make as workable a system as we can of our own morality, taking it as we find it, with an inevitable element of imperfection and error which I hope posterity will correct and supplement, just as we have corrected and supplemented certain errors and deficiencies in the morality of preceding ages.

So again, I hope we shall not waste words on the question of the freedom of the will, so prominent in the writings of some moralists. I do not think that ought to be included among the problems of practical ethics. Whether, and in what sense, we could have realized in the past, or can realize in the future the ideal of rational conduct which we have not realized, is not needed to be known for our present purposes. All we need to assume—and I suppose we may assume this of persons joining an Ethical Society—is that they have a desire of a certain force to realize their common moral ideal, and that they think it will help them to get their conception of it clearer.

And this leads me to another topic, more difficult to excise, but which yet I should like to omit. When we try to get the conception of rational conduct clear we come upon the "double nature of Good," which, as Bacon tells us, is "formed in everything"; we are met with the profound difficulty of harmonizing the good of the individual with the good of the larger whole of which he is a part or member. In my professional treatment of ethics I have concerned myself much with this question,—considering it to be the gravest formal defect of the Utilitarianism of Mill and Bentham, under whose influence my own view was formed, that it treats this problem so inadequately. But I do not want to introduce it into the discussions of our Society; I should prefer to assume—what I think we are all prepared to assume—that each of us wants to do what is best for the larger whole of which he is a part, and that it is not our business to supply him with egoistic reasons for doing it. In saying this, I do not dispute his claim to be supplied with such reasons by any moralist professing to construct a complete ethical system. When J. S. Mill says, in the peroration of a powerful address, "I do not attempt to stimulate you with the prospect of direct rewards, either earthly or heavenly; the less we think about being rewarded in either way the better for us," I think it is a hard saying, too hard for human nature. The demand that happiness shall be connected with virtue cannot be finally quelled in this way; but for the purposes of our Society I am ready to adopt, and should prefer to adopt, Mill's position.

And this leads me naturally to a point of very practical moment—the relation of our Society to the Christian Churches. For one great function of the religious teaching of the Churches—in all ages—has been the supply of extra-mundane motives stimulating men to the performance of duty. Such motives have been both of higher and lower kinds, appealing respectively to different elements of our nature—fears of hell-fire and outer darkness, of wailing and gnashing of teeth, for the brutal and selfish element in us, that can hardly be kept down without these coarse restraints; while to our higher part it has been shown how heavenly love in saints has fused into one the double nature of good; how—like earthly love in its moments of intensity—it has "Touched the chord of self that trembling passed in music out of sight." Well, in all this—if my view be adopted—the Ethical Society will make no attempt to compete with the Churches. We shall contemplate the relation of virtue to the happiness of the virtuous agent, as we believe it actually to be in the present world, and not refer to any future world in which we may hope for compensation for the apparent injustices of the present. And in thus limiting ourselves to mundane motives we shall, I hope, keep a middle path between optimism and pessimism. That is, we shall not profess to prove that the apparent sacrifices of self-interest which duty imposes are never in the long run real sacrifices; nor, on the other hand, shall we ignore or underrate the noble and refined satisfactions which experience shows to attend the resolute choice of virtue in spite of all such sacrifices—

> *"The stubborn thistles bursting*
> *Into glossy purples, which outredden*
> *All voluptuous garden-roses."*

It may, however, be said that it is not merely the function of Churches to supply motives for the performance of duty, but also to teach what duty is, and that here their work must inevitably coincide—and perhaps clash—with that undertaken by an Ethical Society. My answer would be that there is at least a large region of secular duty in which thoughtful Christians commonly recognize that an ideal of conduct can be, and ought to be, worked out by the light of reason independently of revelation; and I should recommend our Society to confine its attention to this secular region. Here no doubt some of us may pursue the quest of moral truth by study or discussion in a non-religious spirit, others in a religious spirit; but I conceive that we have room for both. As a Society, I conceive that our attitude ought to be at once unexclusive as regards the non-religious, and unaggressive as regards all forms of Christian creed.

In saying this, I keep in view the difficulty that many feel in separating at all the ideas of morality and religion, and I have no wish to sharpen the distinction. Indeed, I myself can hardly conceive a working Ethical Society of which the aim would not include in essentials the apostle's definition of the pure service of religion. We might characterize it as the aim of being in the world and yet not of it, working strenuously for the improvement of mundane affairs, and yet keeping ourselves, as the apostle says, "unspotted of the world"—that is, in modern phrase, keeping clear of the compromises with sordid interests and vulgar ambitions which the practical standards of all classes and sections of society are too apt to admit. Of such compromises I will say a word presently: my point now is that the maintenance of an ideal in this sense unworldly must be the concern of any Ethical Society worthy of the name, nor do I see why those who habitually contemplate this ideal from a religious point of view should be unable to co-operate with those who habitually contemplate it from as purely ethical point of view. I do not say that there are no difficulties in such co-operation; but I am sure that we all bring with us a sincere desire to minimize these difficulties, and if so, I do not see why they should not be avoided or overcome.

To sum up: the region in which we are to move I conceive as, philosophically, a middle region, the place of intermediate ethical generalizations which we are content to conceive in a rough and approximate way, avoiding fundamental controversies as far as we can; while from a religious point of view it is a secular but not therefore irreligious region, in which we pursue merely mundane ends, but yet not in a worldly spirit.

But it remains to define more clearly its relation to particular practical problems. In the present age it is impossible that any group of educated persons, spontaneously constituted by their common interest in practical ethics, should not have their attention prominently drawn to the numerous schemes of social improvement on which philanthropic effort is being expended. In this way we may be easily led in our ethical discussions to debate one after another such practical questions as, "Shall we work for State-aided emigration, or promote recreative education, or try to put down sweating? Shall we spend our money in providing open spaces for the poor, or our leisure on a Charity Organization Committee?" Now I have no doubt myself that persons of education, especially if they have comparative wealth and leisure, ought to interest themselves in some or all of these things; and I think it belongs to us in Cambridge, not only to diffuse a general conviction of the importance of this kind of work, but also to encourage a searching examination of the grounds on which particular schemes are urged on the public attention. But in this examination a detailed study of social facts necessarily comes in along with the study of principles, and—though I have no wish to draw a hard and fast line—I should be disposed to regard this study of facts as lying in the main beyond the province of our Society, whose attention should be rather concentrated on principles. I should propose to leave it to some economic or philanthropic association to examine how far an alleged social want exists, and how urgent it is, and by what particular methods it may best be satisfied or removed. What we have rather to consider is how far the eleemosynary or philanthropic intervention of private outsiders in such cases is in accordance with a sound general view of the relation of the individual to his society. It is with the general question, "What social classes owe to each other," that we are primarily concerned, though in trying to find the right answer to this question we may obtain useful instruction from a consideration of the particular fields of work to which I have referred.

But the moral problem offered by the social relations of different classes—though specially prominent in the thought of the present age—is not the only problem causing practical perplexities that such discussions as ours might reduce. There are many other such problems in our complicated modern life—even omitting those obviously unfit for public oral discussion. One class of them which specially interests me is presented by the divergence of the current practical standards of particular sections of the community, on certain points, from the common moral ideal which the community as a whole still maintains. We feel that such divergences are to a great extent an evil, the worldliness which we have to avoid; but yet we think them in some degree legitimate, and the difficulty lies in drawing the line. Any careful discussion of such deflections must lead to what bears the unpopular name of Casuistry. I think, however, that the odium which in the seventeenth century overwhelmed the systematic discussion by theologians of difficult and doubtful cases of morals—though undeniably in part deserved—went to an unreasonable length, and obscured the real importance of the study against which it was directed. There is no doubt that individuals are strongly tempted to have recourse to casuistry in order to find excuses for relaxing in their own favour the restraints of moral rules which they find inconvenient; and hence a casuist has come to be regarded with suspicion as a moralist who aims at providing his clients with the most plausible excuses available for this purpose. But though certain casuists have been reasonably suspected of this misapplication of their knowledge and ingenuity, the proper task of casuistry has always been quite different; the question with which it has properly been concerned is how far, in the particular circumstances of certain classes of persons, the common good demands a special interpretation or modification of some generally accepted moral rule. This, at any rate, is the kind of casuistical problem that I have now in view: and I think that any morality that refuses to deal with such problems must confess itself inadequate for the practical guidance of men engaged in the business of the world; since modifications of morality to meet the special needs of special classes are continually claimed, and more or less admitted by serious and well-meaning persons. Thus it is widely held that barristers must be allowed to urge persuasively for their clients considerations that they know to be false or misleading; that a clergyman may be a most virtuous man without exactly believing the creeds he says or the articles he signs; that a physiologist must be allowed to torture innocent animals; that a general in war must be allowed to use spies and at the same time to hang the spies of the conflicting general. I do not say that most educated persons would accept broadly all these relaxations, but that they would at least admit some of them more or less. Especially in the action of states or governments as such is this kind of divergence admitted, though vaguely and rather reluctantly. When Pope asked—using the names of two noted criminals:

> Is it for Bond or Peter, paltry things,
> To pay their debts or keep their faith like kings?

the epigram was undeniably deserved: still we do not commonly think that governments are bound to keep their faith quite like private individuals; we do not think that repudiating a treaty between nation and nation is quite like breaking a promise between man and man. On all these and similar points I think it would be of real practical utility if discussion could help us to clearer views. For there is a serious danger that when the need of such relaxations is once admitted they may be carried too far; that, in the esoteric morality of any particular profession or trade, ordinary morality will be put aside altogether on certain particular questions, as the opinion of ignorant outsiders; and no result could be more unfavourable than this to the promotion of ethical interests.

So far I have been speaking of particular and limited conflicts between what may be called sectional morality and general morality. But there are departments of society and life of which the relation to ethics is perplexing in a more broad and general way, just because of the elevated and ideal character of their aims—I mean art and science. The practical maxims of some classes of artists and scientific men are liable to collide with common morality in the manner just mentioned—e.g., certain painters or novelists may deliberately disregard the claims of sexual purity—but it is not of these limited conflicts that I now wish to speak, but of the perplexity one finds in fixing the general relation of the ends of Art and Science to moral ends. Perhaps it will be impossible to deal with this without falling into the metaphysical controversies that I have abjured; but the problem often presents itself to me entirely apart from the questions of the schools. When I surrender myself to the pursuit of truth or the impressions of art, I find myself in either case in a world absorbing and satisfying to my highest nature, in which, nevertheless, morality seems to occupy a very subordinate place, and in which—for the more effective realization of the aesthetic or scientific ideal—it seems necessary that morality should be thus subordinated. The difficulty seems to be greater in the case of the aesthetic ideal, because the emotional conflict is greater. The lover of truth has to examine with neutral curiosity the bad and the good in this mixed world, in order to penetrate its laws; but he need not sympathize with the bad or in any way like its existence. But this is harder for the lover of beauty: since evil—even moral evil—is an element in the contrasts and combinations that give him the delight of beauty. If, as Renan says, such a career as Cesar Borgia's is "beautiful as a tempest or an abyss," it is difficult for a lover of beauty not to rejoice that there was a Cesar Borgia. One may even say that in proportion as the sentiment of beauty becomes absorbing and quasi-religious, this divergence from morality is liable to become more marked: because what is bad in a picturesque and exciting way comes to be more and more felt as discord art-fully harmonized in the music that all things make to God.

Well, is this feeling in any degree legitimate? and if so, how is it to be reconciled with our moral aspirations? I do not expect to attain a single cogently-reasoned answer, which all must accept, to either of these questions. They will probably always be somewhat differently answered by different sets and schools of thoughtful persons. But I think they may illustrate the kind of questions on which we may hope to clear up our ideas and reduce the extent of our mutual disagreement by frank and sympathetic discussion.

[The limits above suggested were thought to be too narrow by the leading spirits of the London Ethical Society. Accordingly, as the reader will see, in the next address—delivered as President of the latter body—I tried to adapt my general view of the nature of the work that such a society might profitably undertake to a wider conception of its scope.]

II

THE AIMS AND METHODS OF
AN ETHICAL SOCIETY

I N taking this opportunity, which your committee has given me, of addressing the London Ethical Society, in the honourable but gravely responsible position of their president, I have thought that I could best fulfil the duties of my station by laying before you one or two difficulties which have occurred to my mind, in thinking how we are to realize the declared aims of our Society on the basis of its declared principles. I hope, indeed, not merely to put forward difficulties, but to offer at least a partial solution of them; but I am conscious that it is easier to raise questions than to settle them, and that there is a danger lest the effect of my remarks may be to repel some minds from the study which we are combined to promote. Still, after anxious thought, I have determined to face this danger. For I do not think we ought to conceal from ourselves that the task we have proposed to our Society is one of which the complete accomplishment is likely to be very difficult. Indeed, were it otherwise, it would hardly have been left for us to accomplish.

An address delivered to the London Ethical Society on April 23, 1893, and published in the *International Journal of Ethics,* October, 1893, under the title "My Station and its Duties."

I will begin by explaining that the difficulties of which I am to speak only affect a part of the aims and work of our Society; there is another part—and a most important part—which they do not affect. The first and most comprehensive of the aims that we have stated is "to assist individual and social efforts after right living." Now, what are the obstacles to right living? Why does not each of us completely fulfil the duties of his station?

First, I put aside such obstacles as may seem to lie in external circumstances and material conditions. I do not mean that such circumstances and conditions may not *cause* the gravest hindrances to right living, which a Society like ours should make the most earnest efforts to remove. But important as it is to diminish these hindrances, it is no less important for an ethical society to lay stress on the old truth—sometimes apt to be overlooked in ardent efforts for economic improvement—that it is possible to act rightly under any material conditions. On this point I need hardly say that there is an overwhelming agreement among moralists. The ancient thinkers went too far, no doubt, in saying that a perfectly wise and good man would be perfectly happy in the extremest tortures. We moderns cannot go so far as that; but we must still maintain, as a cardinal and essential ethical truth, that a perfectly wise and good man could behave rightly even under these painful conditions. In short, the immediate obstacles to right conduct, however they may be caused, lie in our minds and hearts, not in our circumstances.

Looking closer at these obstacles, we find that they lie partly in the state of our intellect, partly in the state of our desires and will. Partly we know our duty imperfectly, partly our motives for acting up to what we know are not strong enough to prevail over our inclination to do something else. The two kinds of obstacles are essentially different, and must be dealt with by different methods; each method has its own problems, and the problems require very different treatment. In what I am to say today I shall treat mainly of the intellectual obstacles—the imperfection of knowledge. But before I proceed to this I will illustrate the manner in which the two obstacles are combined, by recalling an anecdote from the early history of ethics. It is told of Socrates that he once met a professional teacher of Wisdom, who informed him that he had discovered the true definition of Justice. "Indeed," said Socrates, "then we shall have no more disputes among citizens about rights and wrongs, no more fights of civic factions, no more quarrels and wars between nations. It is, indeed, a most magnificent discovery!"

Now, the first impression that this remark makes on us is that Socrates is speaking ironically, as no doubt he partly is. We know that men and nations continually commit injustice knowingly; we remember the old fable of the wolf and the lamb—where the wolf pleads his own cause, and then pronounces and immediately executes sentence of capital punishment on the weaker animal—and we surmise that the practical result of this famous debate would not have been altered by our supplying the wolf with the clearest possible formula of justice; the argument might have been cut short, but it would have been all the same in the end to the lamb.

But let us look at the matter again, and we shall see that the master's meaning is not entirely ironical. Let us suppose that our notion of justice suddenly became so clear that in every conflict that is now going on between individuals and classes and nations, every instructed person could at once see what justice required with the same absolute certainty and exactness with which a mathematician can now see the answer to a problem in arithmetic; so that if might anywhere overbore right, it would have to be mere naked brutal force, without a rag of moral excuse to hide its nakedness; suppose this, and I think we see at once that though all the injustice in the world would not come to an end—since there is a good deal of the wolf still left in man—yet undoubtedly there would be much less injustice; we should still want policemen and soldiers, but we should have much less occasion for their services.

Now, let us make a different supposition: let us suppose the state of our knowledge about justice unchanged, but all the obstacles on the side of motive removed; let us suppose that men's ideas of their rights are still as confused and conflicting as they are now, but that every one is filled with a predominant desire to realize justice, strong enough to prevail over every opposing inclination. Here again we must admit that we should not thus get rid of injustice altogether. I am afraid that it would still be true, as the poet says, that

> *New and old, disastrous feud,*
> *Must ever shock like armed foes,*

and we must still look to have serious and even sanguinary conflicts between nations and parties, conscientiously inscribing on their banners conflicting principles of Right. But though unintentional injustice of the gravest kind might still be done, what a relief it would be to humanity to have got rid of all intended wrong; and how much nobler, less exasperating, more chivalrous, would be the conflicts that still had to go on, if each combatant knew that his adversary was fighting with perfect rectitude of purpose.

I have laid stress on this comparison of imaginary improvements, because I think that those who are earnestly concerned for the moral amelioration of themselves and others are often apt to attend too exclusively to one or other of the two sets of obstacles that I have distinguished. They are either impressed with the evils of moral ignorance, and think that if anyone really *knew* what the good life was, he must live it; or, what is more common, they are too exclusively occupied with the defects of desire and will, and inclined to say that anyone knows his duty well enough if he would only act up to his knowledge. Now, I hope we shall agree that an ethical society worthy of the name must aim at removing both kinds of defects; success in both endeavours is necessary for the complete accomplishment of our task; but as success in either is difficult, it may encourage us somewhat to think how much would be gained by success in only one of these endeavours, even if the other is supposed to fail altogether. In the education of the young and in the practical work of our Society the aim of developing the motives to right action, of intensifying the desire for the good life, must always be prominent. This endeavour has its own difficulties and dangers of failure, and I do not propose to deal with them today. But before I pass on to my special subject—the other endeavour to remove the defects of moral knowledge—may I say one thing, out of my observation of human life, as to the endeavour I leave on one side. Though the gift of inspiring enthusiasm for duty and virtue is like other gifts, very unequally distributed among well-meaning persons, I do not believe that anyone who had himself an ardent love of goodness ever failed entirely to communicate it to others. He may fail in his particular aims, he may use ill-devised methods, meet with inexplicable disappointments, make mistakes which cause him bitter regret; but we shall find that after all, though the methods may have failed, the man has succeeded; somewhere, somehow, in some valuable degree, he has—if I may use an old classical image—handed on the torch of his own ardour to others who will run the race for the prize of virtue.

We are agreed, then, that much may be done if we simply take the current ideal of what is right, and earnestly endeavour to develop a desire to realize it in ourselves and others. But this is not the whole of our aim. We are conscious of defects in this current ideal, and it is impossible for us really to care for it and at the same time to sit down content with these defects. Hence we state it as our second aim "to free the current ideal of what is right from all that is merely traditional and self-contradictory, and thus to widen and perfect it."

With this view we invite all our members "to assist in constructing a Theory or Science of Right, which, starting with the reality and validity of moral distinctions, shall explain their mental and social origin, and connect them in a logical system of thought."

It is to the difficulties involved in the task thus defined that my thoughts have chiefly turned in meditating what I was to say to you today.

I think that no instructed person can regard it as other than arduous. Speaking broadly, what we propose to do is what ancient thinkers had been trying to do for many centuries, before the Christian churches monopolized the work of moralizing mankind in this quarter of the globe; and it is also what a long line of modern thinkers have been trying to do for several centuries more, since independent ethical thought revived in Europe, after the long mediæval period of submission to ecclesiastical authority.

Yet the phrase we use—"assist in constructing"—implies that after all these efforts the construction yet remains to be effected. We must, then, hardly be surprised if we do not find it easy.

Still there is a Greek proverb that says "the fine things are difficult," and I by no means wish to say a word to dissuade anyone from devoting his energies to so noble a cause, especially since a large part of my own life has been spent in working for this end.

And in order that I may be as little discouraging as possible, I will begin with a difficulty which seems to me sufficiently important to be worth discussing, but which I hope to be able to remove completely.

At first sight it might seem as if the task that we have undertaken, the task of "explaining the mental and social origin of moral distinctions, and connecting them in a logical system of thought," was one that could only be carried out by experts—i.e., by persons who have gone through a thorough training in psychology, sociology, and logic—in short, by philosophers. But the plan on which our Society has been framed—and I believe the same is true of all other ethical societies which have been founded—invites the co-operation of all thoughtful persons who sympathize with its principles and aims, whether they are experts in psychology and sociology or not. And if our movement succeeds, the element of non-experts is evidently likely largely to outnumber the experts, unless the philosophers of the community should increase in number more than is to be expected, or perhaps even desired.

The question then arises, can this unphilosophic majority really aid in the task of constructing a Theory of Right which shall eliminate error and contradiction from current morality, reduce all valid moral perceptions and judgments to their elements or first principles, and present them as connected in a logical system of thought? Ought we not, at least, to divide and distribute our task more clearly and thoroughly? Does not our invitation at present seem to hand over a work of intellectual construction, requiring the highest gifts and the completest training, to persons who are not, and who cannot be expected to become, duly qualified for the work? Will not these untrained builders build with untempered mortar?

I have stated this difficulty plainly, because I at first felt it strongly myself, and therefore think that others may have felt it. But reflection convinced me that if your society has been right—and I hope experience may show that it has been right—in undertaking the noble but arduous task which it has proposed to itself, there is much to be said for the broad and comprehensive basis which it has adopted. There are serious reasons for thinking that the work undertaken cannot be thoroughly well done by philosophers alone; partly because alone they are not likely to have the requisite knowledge of facts; and partly because their moral judgment on any particular question of duty, even supposing them to have obtained all available information as to the particular facts of the case, is not altogether to be trusted, unless it is aided, checked, and controlled by the moral judgment of persons with less philosophy but more special experience.

First, as I say, the philosopher's knowledge is likely to be inadequate for the accomplishment of our aim. Our aim is to frame an ideal of the good life for humanity as a whole, and not only for some particular section; and to do this satisfactorily and completely we must have adequate knowledge of the conditions of this life in all the bewildering complexity and variety in which it is actually being lived. This necessity is imposed on us by the modern ethical ideal which our Western civilization owes to Christianity. We cannot any longer decline—as Aristotle would have declined—to work out an ideal of good life for mechanics and tradesmen, on the ground that such persons are incapable of any high degree of virtue. But if we are to frame an ideal of good life for all, and to show how a unity of moral spirit and principle may manifest itself through the diversity of actions and forbearances, efforts and endurances, which the diversity of social functions renders necessary—we can only do this by a comprehensive and varied knowledge of the actual opportunities and limitations, the actual needs and temptations, the actually constraining customs and habits, desires and fears, of all the different species of that "general man" who, as Browning says, "receives life in parts to live in a whole." And this knowledge a philosopher—whose personal experience is often very limited—cannot adequately attain unless he earnestly avails himself of opportunities of learning from the experience of men of other callings.

But, secondly, even supposing him to have used these opportunities to the full, the philosopher's practical judgment on particular problems of duty is liable to be untrustworthy, unless it is aided and controlled by the practical judgment of others who are not philosophers. This may seem to some a paradox. It may be thought that so far as a philosopher has a sound general theory of right, he must be able to apply it to determine the duties of any particular station in life, if he has taken due pains to inform himself as to that station and its circumstances. And this would doubtless be true if his information could be made complete; but this it cannot be. He can only learn from others the facts which they have consciously observed and remembered; but there is an important element in the experience of themselves and their predecessors—the continuous experience of social generations—which finds no place in any statement of facts or reasoned forecast of consequences that they could furnish; it is only represented in their judgments as to what ought to be done and aimed at. Hence it is a common observation that the judgments of practical men as to what ought to be done in particular circumstances are often far sounder than the reasons they give for them; the judgments represent the result of experience unconsciously as well as consciously imbibed; the reasons have to be drawn from that more limited part of experience which has been

of their station, in whatever station they may be found, that the moral philosopher should, as I have said, give reverent attention, in order that he may be aided and controlled by them in his theoretical construction of the Science of Right.

Perhaps some of my audience may think that in what I have just been saying I have been labouring the wrong point; that it needs no argument to show that the moral philosopher, if he tries to work out a reasoned theory of duty by which all the particular duties of particular stations may find their places in one harmonious and coherent system, cannot dispense with the aid and guidance of the special moral experience of practical men; but that what requires to be proved is rather that the practical man, who desires earnestly to know and fulfil the particular duties of his particular station, has any need of the philosopher. And certainly I must admit that there is a widespread opinion, supported by moralists of great repute, that he has hardly any such need; that, as Butler says, "any plain honest man in almost any circumstances, if, before he engages in any course of action, he asked himself, 'Is this I am going about right, or is it wrong?' would answer the question agreeably to truth and virtue." Or if it be granted that such a plain honest man has any need of philosophers, it is said to be only to protect him against other philosophers; it is because there are bad philosophers—what we call sophists—about, endeavouring to undermine and confuse the plain man's naturally clear notions of duty, that there has come to be some need of right-minded thinkers to expose the sophistries and dispel the confusions. It is held, in short, that if any assistance can be obtained from the moral philosopher by a plain man who is making serious efforts after right living, it is not the positive kind of assistance which a physician gives to those who consult him for rules of diet, but a merely negative assistance, such as the policeman gives who warns suspicious characters off the premises.

This view is so often put forward that I cannot but infer that it is really very widely entertained, and that it corresponds to the moral experience of many persons; that many plain honest men really do think that they always know what their duty is—at any rate, if they take care not to confuse their moral sense by bad philosophy. In my opinion such persons are, to some extent, under an illusion, and really know less than they think. But whether I could convince them of this, or whether, if I could convince them, it would be really for their advantage, are questions which I need not now consider, because I think it hardly likely that such persons have joined our Ethical Society in any considerable numbers. For to practical men of this stamp the construction of a theory or science of right must seem a work of purely speculative interest, having no particular value whatever; a work, therefore, which persons who have not studied psychology or sociology had better leave to those who profess these subjects. It is not to plain men of this type that our appeal is made, but rather to those whose reflection has made them aware that in their individual efforts after right living they have often to grope and stumble along an imperfectly-lighted path; whose experience has shown them uncertainty, confusion, and contradiction in the current ideal of what is right, and has thus led them to surmise that it may be liable to limitations and imperfections, even when it appears clear and definite. Practical men of this stamp will recognize that the effort to construct a Theory of Right is not a matter of mere speculative interest, but of the deepest practical import; and they will no more try to dispense with the aid of philosophy than the moral philosopher—if he knows his own limitations—will try to dispense with the aid of moral common sense.

Well, may I say that here is one difficulty removed? But I am afraid that removing it only brings another into view. We have seen how and why philosophers are to co-operate with earnest and thoughtful persons who are not philosophers in constructing an ethical system; but the discussion has made it evident that the main business of construction and explanation—on the basis of psychology and sociology—must be thrown on the philosophers; and then the question arises, how are they to co-operate among themselves? The reason why the work remains to be done lies in the fundamental disagreement that has hitherto existed among philosophers as to the principles and method of ethical construction; and so long as this disagreement continues, how is co-operation possible? Well, I think it may be said on the hopeful side, that there is more willingness now to co-operate than there has been in other times not very remote. Fundamental disagreements on principles and methods can only be removed by systematic controversy; but it was difficult to conduct philosophical controversy in a spirit of mutual aid and co-operation, so long as philosophers had the bad habit of arguing in as exasperated a tone as if each had suffered a personal injury through the publication of views opposed to his own. This bad habit has not nearly passed away, and a glance at the names of our committee will show that moralists of the most diverse philosophical schools are willing to combine in the work of an ethical society. But this willingness does not altogether remove the difficulty, or rather it removes it as regards a part of our aims, but not as regards another part. It is easy to see how philosophers of diverse schools may, by sympathetic efforts at mutual understanding and interpenetration of ideas, assist each other in constructing a theory or science of right; but even under these favourable conditions the labour of this construction is likely to be long, and how, in the meantime—so long as their fundamental disagreements are unremoved—can they effectually combine to assist individual and social efforts after right living? So long as they are not agreed on the ultimate end of action—so long as one holds it to be moral perfection, another "general happiness," another "efficiency of the social organism"—how can any counsels they may combine to give, as to the right way of living so as best to realize the end, be other than discordant and bewildering to those who seek their counsels? The difficulty would be avoided if all the philosophers of the Ethical Society belonged to the same school, for then they could assist those who were not philosophers by reasoned deductions from the accepted principles of the school. They would have to admit that other philosophers held fundamentally different principles, but they would explain to their hearers that the other philosophers were wrong. But, then, if our movement flourished and was found to meet a social need, these other philosophers would be led to form ethical societies of their own. The non-philosophic members of the different societies could not be thoroughly competent judges of the philosophical disputes; but loyalty and *esprit de corps* would lead them to stand firmly by their respective philosophers; and the result must be that any assistance rendered by these competing ethical societies to individual and social efforts after right living would be hampered by the grave drawbacks of sectarian rivalries and conflicts. In short, it seemed to me that the ethical movement was in a dilemma; if each school had its own ethical society, it incurred the dangers of sectarianism; if different schools combined to work in the same society, it incurred the danger of a bewildering discord of counsels.

In this perplexing choice of alternatives, I think that our Society has adopted the right course in accepting the difficulty that attaches to combined efforts; and I think that if this difficulty is contemplated fairly and considerably, though we cannot completely remove it, we can find a pro-visional solution of it sufficient for practical purposes.

I find this solution in the generally-admitted fact, that there is much greater agreement among thoughtful persons on the question what a good life is, than on the question why it is good. When they are trying to define the ultimate end of right actions, the conceptions they re-spectively apply seem to be so widely divergent that the utmost efforts of mutual criticism are hardly sufficient to enable them even to under-stand each other. But when, from the effort to define the ultimate end of right conduct, we pass to discuss right conduct itself, whether viewed on its inner or its outer side—the spirit in which a good life is to be lived, the habits of thought and feeling that it requires, the external man-ifestations of this inner rectitude in the performance of duty and the re-alization of virtue—then the disagreement is reduced to a surprising ex-tent. I do not say that it becomes insignificant, that there is no important difference of opinion among philosophers as to the details and particu-lars of morality. Were this so, the task of an ethical society would be less arduous than I have felt bound to represent it; but it is at any rate not sufficient to prevent a broad, substantial agreement as to the practical ideal of a good life. And I think that philosophers of the most diverse schools may combine on the basis of this broad and general agreement with each other, and with earnest and thoughtful persons who are not philosophers in their practical ideals; and letting their fundamental dif-ferences on ultimate principles drop into the background may hopefully co-coperate in efforts to realize the second of our aims, to free this cur-rent ideal from all that is merely traditional and self-contradictory, and thus to widen and perfect it.

But I am afraid you will think that our task, as I conceive it, is like the climbing of a mountain, of which the peaks are hidden one after another behind lower peaks; for when one difficulty is surmounted it brings an-other into view. We have agreed that our business is to "free the current ideal of what is right from all that is merely traditional"; but we are also agreed—it is one of our express principles—that the good life "is to be realized by accepting and acting in the spirit of such common obligations as are enjoined by the relationships of family and society." But when we look closer at these common obligations, we find that they are actually determined by tradition and custom to so great an extent that, if we subtracted the traditional element, it would be very difficult to say what the spirit of the obligation was. This is not perhaps clear at first sight, because the moral tradition, familiar to us from childhood upward, blends itself so completely with our conception of the facts that it seems to the unreflecting mind to arise out of them naturally and inevitably; but if we take any such common obligation and compare the different conceptions of it as we find them in different ages and countries, the large space occupied by the traditional element becomes clear through the great range of its variations. Take, for instance, the family relations. As we trace these down the stream of time we see them undergoing remarkable changes, both in extent and content. The mutual claims of kindred more remote than the descendants of the same parents or grandparents, which in primitive times are strong and important, become feeble and evanescent as civilization goes on; while within the narrower circle, within which the tie still remains strong, the element of authority on the one hand and of obedience on the other—authority of husbands over wives and parents over children—is subject to a similar, though not an equal, diminution; on the other hand, the interference of the State in the domestic control and provision for children's welfare, which was at first left entirely to parents, is a marked feature of recent social progress. During the whole of this process of historic change the recognized mutual obligations of members of the family have been determined by the actual state of traditional morality at any given time; when, then, from this historic survey we turn to scrutinize our own ideal of family duty, how are we to tell how much of it belongs to mere tradition, which the river of progress will sweep away, and how much belongs to the indestructible conditions of the well-being of life, propagated as human life must be propagated? And the same may be said when we pass from domestic to social and political relations: what social classes owe to each other, according to our commonly-accepted ideal of morality, depends on traditions which result from a gradual development, are going through a process of change, and are actually assailed by doubts and controversies often of a deep and far-reaching kind. How can we find in this moving, though slowly moving, mass of traditional rules and sentiments, which is the element in which our outward moral life is necessarily lived, any stable foundation on which to build, and to invite others to build, the structure of as good life? And yet, on the other hand, we have pledged ourselves not to acquiesce in "mere tradition" when recognized as such, for which indeed we can hardly feel, or hope to inspire, any enthusiasm.

Of this difficulty there is, I think, no complete solution possible, until our task of constructing a theory or science of Right has been satisfactorily accomplished; but some suggestions may be made, helpful towards the provisional solution which we practically require, and with these I will now briefly conclude.

First, the same historic survey which shows us the process of continual change through which human morality has passed also shows us that—like the structures of physical organisms—it tends to be continually adapted, in a subtle and complex manner, to the changing conditions and exigencies of human society. This tendency does not, indeed, suffice to place traditional morality above criticism; since we have no ground for regarding its adaptation to social needs as being at any time perfect, and critical discussion is an indispensable means of improving it. But a contemplation of the profoundly important part played by morality, as it changes and develops along with other elements in the complex fact of social evolution, should make our critical handling of it respectful and delicate, and should quell that temper of rebellion against tradition and convention, into which the reflective mind is apt to fall, in the first reaction against the belief in the absolute validity of current and accepted rules.

Secondly, though the traditional and conventional element of current morality cannot belong to our moral ideal as abstractly contemplated, it may none the less incontrovertibly claim a place in the concrete application of that ideal to present facts. For instance, a refined sense of justice will require us to fulfil the expectations warranted by any implied and tacit understandings into which we may have entered, no less than those which depend on express and definite contracts: and the implied and mutually-understood conditions of our voluntary social relations are in most cases largely determined by tradition and custom. On the other hand, if in reflecting on the morality of our age we find it to contain palpable inconsistencies; if accepted particular rules cannot be reconciled with equally accepted general principles, or tolerated practices reconciled with accepted rules; if there is an arbitrary inequality, based on no rational grounds, in the commonly approved treatment of human beings; if, to take a simple case, we find that we can find no real moral distinction between conduct which we have judged legitimate on our own part towards others and conduct which we have judged illegitimate on the part of others towards us—then in such inconsistencies we may recognize a sure sign of error and need of change in our ethical view.

Thirdly, in considering difficulties of detail we should never lose grasp of the importance of that rectitude of purpose, that mental attitude and habit of devotion to universal good, which constitutes the core and centre of the good life. Whatever else shifts, as life and thought changes, this central element is stable and its moral value indestructible; and it not only consoles us to rest on this certitude when practical doubts and perplexities assail us, but it may sometimes afford a solution of these doubts. It is, indeed, a dangerous error to hold that it does not matter what we do so long as we do it in the right spirit. But though a dangerous error, it is still only an exaggeration of the truth; for there are many cases where it really does not matter very much to ourselves or to others which of two alternative courses we adopt, so long as we take whichever we do take in a spirit of sincere devotion to the general good, and carry it through in the manner and mood of thought and feeling which belong to this spirit.

Further, we may make this old and abstract conception of the general good more full and definite by combining it with the more modern conception of society as an organism: in which each individual worker in any trade or profession is to be regarded as a member of an organ, having his share of responsibility for the action of this organ. We shall thus recognize that the right condition of any such organ depends on the service it renders to the whole organism; so that if the accepted moral rules and sentiments of any such social class are seen to tend to the benefit of the part at the expense of the whole they stand condemned. It does not follow that the rules should be at once set aside—as this might cause a greater evil in the way of disappointment and disturbance—but we must recognize the need of change and begin the process. Similarly, if we find that elements of human good, such as knowledge and art, important in the life of the whole, are not sufficiently recognized in our current moral ideal, the same principle will require us to enlarge and extend this ideal to admit them.

And if it be said that after all is done the moral ideal of our age, however purged of inconsistencies and inspired and expanded by a steady self-devotion to the most comprehensive notion of good that we can form, is still imperfect and mutable; and that it must be expected to undergo, in the future, transformations now unforeseen; it yet need not painfully disturb us that the best of our possessions should be thus subject to the inexorable conditions of mundane existence. It need not hinder us from cherishing and holding to the best we have so long as it remains the best. Life is essentially change, and the good life must be essentially life; it is enough if it contain unchanged amid the change that aspiration after the best life, which is itself a chief source and spring of change.

III

PUBLIC MORALITY

THERE are two distinct ways of treating ethical questions, the difference between which, in respect of method, is fundamental; though it does not necessarily lead to controversy or diversity of systems. We may begin by establishing fundamental principles of abstract or ideal morality, and then proceed to work out deductively the particular rules of duty or practical conceptions of human good or well-being, through the adoption of which these principles may be as far as possible realized, under the actual conditions of human life. Or, we may contemplate morality as a social fact—"positive morality" as it has been called—i.e., the body of opinions and sentiments as to right and wrong, good and evil, which we find actually prevalent in the society of which we are members; and endeavour, by reflective analysis, removing vagueness and ambiguity, solving apparent contradictions, correcting lapses and supplying omissions, to reduce this body of current opinions, so far as possible, to a rational and coherent system. The two methods are in no way antagonistic: indeed, it

An essay read on Jan. 26, 1897, at a meeting of a Cambridge essay-club called "The Eranus."

may reasonably be contended that if pursued with complete success, they must lead to the same goal—a perfectly satisfactory and practical ideal of conduct. But in the actual condition of our intellectual and social development, the respective results of the two methods are apt to exhibit a certain divergence, which, for practical purposes, we have to obliterate—more or less consciously—by a rough compromise.

In the present discourse, I shall adopt primarily the second method. I shall accordingly mean by "public morality" prevalent opinions as to right and wrong in public conduct; that is, primarily in the conduct of governments—whether in relation to the members of the states governed, or in dealings with other states. We must, however, extend the notion, especially in states under popular government, to include opinions as to the conduct of private individuals and associations, so far as they influence or control government; or we might put it otherwise, by saying that in such states every man who possesses the franchise has a share in the functions and responsibilities of government. Thus, in such states the morality of party strife is a department of public morality. The limits of my discourse will compel me to concentrate attention mainly on government in the ordinary sense—the persons primarily responsible for governmental action, and to whose conduct the judgment of right and wrong applies in the first instance. But it seemed desirable to notice at the outset the wider extension of governmental responsibilities that belongs to democracy; because on this largely depends, in my view, not the theoretical interest, but the practicl urgency of the question that I am about to raise.

For the most important inquiry which my subject at the present time suggests is whether there is any deep and fundamental distinction between public and private morality; any more difference, that is, than between the moralities belonging respectively to different professions and callings. We all, of course, recognize that in a certain sense the application of moral rules varies for different professions: certain kinds of duty become specially important for each profession, and accordingly come to be defined for it with special precision; and certain minor problems of conduct are presented to members of one profession which are not presented to another. In this way some variations are thus caused in the practical casuistry belonging to different callings; so that we might speak of clerical morality, legal morality, and medical morality; but in so speaking we should be commonly understood to refer to variations in detail of comparatively minor importance. It would be a violent paradox to maintain that the ordinary rules of veracity, justice, good faith, etc., were suspended wholly or partially in the case of any of these professions. But the case is different with the deaprtment of morality which deals with the conduct of states or governments. In this region paradoxes of the kind just mentioned have been deliberately maintained by so many grave persons that we can hardly refuse them serious attention. Indeed, if anyone will study the remarkable catena of authorities quoted by Lord Acton in his introduction to Burd's edition of Machiavelli's *Prince,* he will, I think, be left in some doubt how far the proposition, that statesmen are not subject in their public conduct even to the most fundamental rules of private morality, can properly be called paradoxical any longer, for persons duly instructed in modern history, and modern political thought. It is still, no doubt, a paradox to the vulgar. It is not a proposition that a candidate for Parliament would affirm on a public platform; but the extent to which it is adopted, explicitly or implicitly, by educated persons is already sufficient to introduce into popular morality an element of perplexity and disturbance, which it would be desirable, if possible, to remove; and this perplexity and disturbance must be expected to increase, in proportion as democracy increases the responsibility—and the sense of responsibility— of the ordinary citizen.

Observe that in speaking of "morality" I have in view the standard by which men are *judged,* not the standard of their practice. It is not merely that the statesman frequently violates the rules of duty, for that we all do. Nor is it merely that, in view of the greatness of his temptations or the nobleness of his patriotic motives, more indulgence is shown to his breaches of justice, veracity, or good faith, than would be shown to similar transgressions in private life; that the historian is "a little blind" to the faults of a man who has rendered valuable services to his country. For this kind of indulgence is also sometimes shown to persons in other vocations, when subject to special temptations or moved by fine impulses; but it does not commonly amount to a modification of the rule by which men are judged, but only to an alteration in the weight of the censure attached to a breach of the rule. Thus public opinion is indulgent to the amorous escapades of gallant soldiers and sailors, though it would condemn similar conduct severely in schoolmasters; but no one would gravely argue that the Seventh Commandment is not binding on military men. So again, we all sympathize with the Jacobite servant who "would rather trust his soul in God's hands than his master in the hands of the Whigs," and therefore committed perjury to avoid the worse alternative; but our sympathy does not lead us to contend that domestic loyalty has a licence to swear falsely on suitable occasions.

Nor, further, is the fact I am considering merely that there is, or has been, an esoteric professional morality current among politicians, in which considerable relaxations are allowed of the ordinary rules of veracity, justice, and good faith. This is doubtless a part of the fact; but if this were all, it would be easy to find analogies for it in several other professions and callings, which are all liable to similar esoteric relaxations of ordinary morality. For instance, I suppose that there is now an esoteric morality widely spread among retail traders which allows of secret payments to cooks and butlers in order to secure their custom; but we do not hear the bribery approved or defended outside the circles of retial tradesmen and domestic servants. So, again, it would seem that in certain ages and countries the current morality among priests has regarded "pious fraud" as legitimate; but the success of this method of promoting the cause of religion would seem to depend upon its being kept strictly esoteric; and I am not aware that it was ever openly defended in works published for the edification of the laity. The peculiarity of the divergence of political from ordinary morality is that it has been repeatedly thus defended, not only by the statesmen themselves, but by literary persons contemplating the statesman's work in the disengaged attitude of students of life and society.

Nor, finally, is it merely that the statesman's breaches of morality, if successful, are liable to be approved by the popular sentiment of the nation which profits by them, so that the writers of this nation are inadvertently led into fallacies and sophistries in order to justify the immoralities in question. This doubtless occurs, and cannot much surprise us. Adam Smith has explained how conscience—the imaginary impartial spectator within the breast of each of us—"requires often to be awakened and put in mind of his duty by the presence of the real spectator"; and how, when the real spectator at hand is interested and partial, while the impartial ones are at a distance, the propriety of moral sentiments is apt to be corrupted. No doubt this partly explains the low state of international morality, and of the morality of party warfare, as compared with ordinary private morality; but this explanation will not suffice to account for the divergence that I am now considering. It is not merely that particular cases in which leading statesmen have employed immoral means for patriotic ends are sophistically defended by patriotic contemporaries belonging to the same nation. The point is that the approval of such breaches if formulated in explicit general maxims, raised into a system, and deliberately applied by eminent students of history and political science to the acts of statesmen in remote ages and countries. This seems to be especially the case in Germany, where men of letters have in recent times taken the lead in advocating the emancipation of the statesman from the restraints of ordinary morality. It is not merely that the German defends his Frederic or his Bismarck to the best of his ability; his historical and philosophical soul is not content with that. To do him justice, he is equally earnest in defending the repudiation by Rome of the treaty with the Samnites after the incident of the Caudine Forks,—or any similar act of bad faith or aggression perpetrated by that remarkably successful commonwealth.

Let us contemplate more closely the principles of this charter of liberation from the ordinary rules of morality, issued to statesmen and states by respectable thinkers of our century. And, first, I may begin by distinguishing the explicitly anti-moral propositions that I have in view from other propositions in some measure cognate, which yet do not definitely imply them. For instance, when a writer speaks of the "irresistible logic of facts," or tells us that history furnishes the only touchstone for political ideals, that great designs and great enterprises can only prove themselves such by succeeding, that achievement is the only criterion of the true statesman, etc., etc.—this does not necessarily imply the emancipation of the statesman from ordinary moral restraints. It may merely mean that the construction of the finest possible Utopia is not statesmanship, and that the true statesman's ideas must be adapted for realization with the means at his disposal and under given conditions; it need not be taken to deny that the restraints of common morality are among these conditions. No doubt this kind of language strongly *suggests* the *"Si possis rectè si non quocunque modo"* of Horace; but though it suggests this meaning, it does not strictly justify us in attributing it to the writer. For one might similarly say that the possession of the art of medicine can only be proved by success, and that the one business of the physician is to cure his patient, without intending to imply that it does not matter what commandments the physician may break, provided only the cure is effected.

So, again, when it is said that morality varies from age to age, and from country to country, that the code shifts with the longitude and alters with the development of society, and that in judging any statesman we must apply the standard of his age and country,—all this seems directed rather to the emancipation of the historian from moral narrowness in his judgments than to the emancipation of the statesman from moral restraint in his conduct. For this language assumes that the statesman *is* bound by the established moral code of his society; it only points out that that court for the award of praise and blame, in which the historian from time to time appoints himself to sit as judge and jury, is subject to the difficulties arising from the diversity and conflict of laws, and that the judicious historian must take care to select and apply the right code. Whether this view is sound or not, it has no logical connection with the doctrine that sets a statesman free from the fundamental rules of morality, recognized as binding in his own age and country.

One more distinction, and then I come to the point. I suppose that if there is any one historic name with which this anti-moral doctrine is to be specially connected, it is the name of Machiavelli; I might indeed have referred to it briefly as "Machiavellianism," only that I am anxious to examine it rather in its nineteenth-century than its sixteenth-century form. Now, competent historians of thought have regarded it as the essential principle of Machiavelli that "the end justifies the means"; and certainly this principle is expressly laid down by the great Florentine, not only in the paradoxical and variously interpreted *Prince,* but in the more moderate and straightforward *Discourses on Livy,*—which have largely escaped the reprobation piled on the more famous treatise. He lays this principle down in treating of a case so remote from modern interest as the slaying of Remus by Romulus; he admits that this fratricide was objectionable in itself, but holds it justified when we take Romulus' ends into account. "A good result excuses any violence." And probably for ordinary readers this statement sufficiently characterizes Machiavelli's doctrine as anti-moral; but it must be obvious that it cannot so characterize it for those who, like myself, hold that the only true basis for morality is a utilitarian basis. I desire here to digress as little as may be into this controversy of the schools: but I must refer to it to avoid confusion and misunderstanding. For in the view of utilitarians the proposition that "the end justifies the means" cannot possibly be taken to characterize the anti-moral position of Machiavelli or his nineteenth-century followers. In our view the end must always ultimately justify the means—there is no other way in which the use of any means whatever could possibly be justified. Only it must be a *universal end;* not the preservation of any particular state, still less its aggrandisement or the maintenance of its existing form of government; but the happiness or well-being of humanity at large—or, rather, of the whole universe of living things, so far as any practical issue can be raised between these two conceptions of the universal end. According to us, then, the immorality of Machiavellianism does not lie in its affirmation that the bindingness of all moral rules is relative, or that the moral value of actions is to be estimated by their consequences—if only a sufficiently wide view is taken of these consequences. It only begins when the end in view and the regard for consequences is narrowed and restricted; when the interest of a particular state is taken as the ultimate and paramount end, justifying the employment of any means whatever to attain it, whatever the consequences of such action may be to the rest of the human race.

And this "national egoism" is, I think, the essence of the Neo-Machiavellianism, which,—though views somewhat similar have frequently found expression from the sixteenth century onward,—has been especially prominent in the political thought of the last forty years, and, as I have said, has found the most unreserved and meditated expression in the writings of Germans. I may give as an example the statements of an able and moderate writer, who is by no means an admirer of Machiavelli. "The state," says Rümelin,★ "is self-sufficient." "Self-regard is its appointed duty; the maintenance and development of its own power and well-being,—egoism, if you like to call this egoism,—is the supreme principle of all politics." "The state can only have regard to the interest of any other state so far as this can be identified with its own interest." "Self-devotion is the principle for the individual, self-assertion for the state." "The maintenance of the state justifies every sacrifice, and is superior to every moral rule."

★ These sentences are taken from an address, "Ueber das Verhältniss der Politik zur Morale," published in 1875, among the *Reden und Aufsätze* of Gustro Rümelin, Chancellor of the University of Tübingen.

It may perhaps be said that this adoption of national interest as a paramount end does not necessarily involve a collision with established morality: that it may be held along with a belief that veracity, good faith, and justice are always the best policy for states and for individuals. But the common sense of Christendom does not affirm this of individuals, if mundane consequences alone are taken into account: and though Bentham and an important section of his earlier followers were prepared to base private morality on pure self-interest empirically ascertained and measured, this doctrine has few defenders now. And the corresponding doctrine as regards national interest is certainly not to be attributed to the German writers to whom I refer: their practical aim in affirming national egoism is almost always expressly to emancipate the public action of statesmen from the restraints of private morality.

The origin of this Neo-Machiavellianism may be traced to various causes. It is partly due to a reaction from the political idealism of the later eighteenth century—a reaction in which moral rules have been thrown overboard along with constitutional principles; partly to a reaction from the cosmopolitanism of the same period, tending to an exaggerated affirmation of the self-sufficiency and absolute moral independence of the nation-state; partly, perhaps, to a kind of Neo-paganism, striving to make patriotism take the place of Christianity. Partly it seems to be connected with the triumph of the historical method, influenced in its earlier state by the Hegelian change of Idealism through Optimism into its opposite, summed up in the famous declaration that the Real is Rational; from which it seems an obvious inference that the man who succeeds is always in the right, whatever his path to success, the man who fails always in the wrong. In any case, I think the nineteenth century study of history has tended to enlarge and systematize the demand for the moral emancipation of the statesman. Doubtless from the time of Machiavelli downwards it has been a common view of practical politicians that "good men" are unsuited for political crises, because they will not, as Walpole puts it, "go the necessary lengths." But so long as Traditional and Ideal Legitimacy were carrying on their constitutional struggle with confident conviction on both sides, the required relaxation from moral restraints was commonly limited to crises sincerely believed to be exceptional. "Revolutions and wars are not made with rose water," said the political idealist; "but when once we have emancipated nations, and established in them free and equal democratic governments, revolutions and wars will be things of the past." "We have to violate rules of right to defend the right," said the party of order, "in the present tempest of revolutionary madness; but, once the madness is over, the powers ordained of God will, of course, conform to the moral order which they are essentially required to maintain." But the convictions of both parties belong to a stage which the movement of nineteenth century thought has now left behind it. The study of history has caused the view to prevail that "the great world" is to "spin for ever down the ringing grooves of change"; and, consequently, at every turn of this rotatory movement forward, there would seem likely to be an ever recurrent need for the morally emancipated statesman—the statesman who, when circumstances drive him to cruelty, rapacity, breach of faith, falsehood, will not waver and whine about the "painful necessity"; but, with simple decision, unhampered by scruples, take the course that leads straightest to the next stage of the everlasting progress.

In the extreme form which this doctrine not unfrequently assumes, and in which I have, for clearness, presented it, it neither invites nor requires a formal refutation; since it neither appeals to the common moral consciousness of mankind, which, indeed, it frankly claims to override, nor to any principles which have ever been accepted by philosophers. For egoism pure and simple, the doctrine that each individual's interest must be for him ultimately paramount to all other considerations, there is, in abstract ethical discussion, much to be said; but I have never seen, nor can I conceive, any ethical reasoning that will provide even a plausible basis for the compound proposition that a man is bound to sacrifice his private interest to that of the group of human beings constituting his state, but that neither he nor they are under any similar obligation to the rest of mankind. And to do them justice, the advocates of this doctrine do not commonly resort to ethical deductions to justify their position. They prefer to appeal to facts; and certainly it is not difficult to find examples of statesmen who have attained their ends by such breaches of current morality as this doctrine defends: but obviously no appeal to facts can settle the question of right without a palpable *petitio principii*.

There is, however, one objection that may be taken to this doctrine on the purely historical ground on which its advocates usually argue. I do not think that the history of polity and of political ideas gives us any reason for believing that this emancipation from morality, if once admitted, will stop where the Neo-Machiavellians desire it to stop—at national egoism. The moral emancipation allowed to governments for the promotion of the interests of the nation will be used by governments for the maintenance of their power, even against the interests of the nation; the distinction between what may be done to hold power and what may be done to acquire it will come to be recognized as arbitrary; and so by an easy inclined plane we shall pass from the Machiavellianism of the *Discourses on Livy* to the Machiavellianism of the *Prince*. Or, again, granting that some kind of corporate sentiment is maintained, there is still no ground for confidence that it will always attach itself to the particular corporation called the state. If everything is permitted in national struggles for the sake of the nation, it will be easy to think that everything is permitted in party-struggles or class-struggles for the sake of the party or class. The tendencies of modern democracy are running strongly towards the increase of corporate sentiments and the habits of corporate action in industrial groups and classes, and so towards dividing civilized humanity by lines that cut across the lines separating nations; and history certainly does not justify us in confidently expecting that when the rules of private morality are no longer held to apply to public action, patriotism will still keep class feeling and party feeling within the bounds required by national peace and well-being. It is in the later period of free Greece—the civilized fourth century—that the class conflict is most disintegrative, which makes, as Plato says, "two cities in one, the city of the rich and the city of the poor": and similarly in mediæval Italy, whereas in the twelfth century the chronicle ran simply, "Parma fights Piacenza," before the end of the thirteenth it ran, "Parma, with the exiles from Piacenza, fights Piacenza."

I conclude, then, that this Neo-Machiavellian doctrine is really condemned by history—the Cæsar to which it appeals—no less than by the old-fashioned moral philosophy that it despises. But I am far from wishing to dismiss it with a bare negation. The extent to which it has found favour with thoughtful persons affords a *prima facie* presumption that there are elements of sound reason in it, which have been exaggerated into dangerous paradox; and, if so, it seems very desirable to get these clear. The most important of these elements—especially as regards international conduct—is, I think, more easily discernible in the work of Hobbes than in that of Machiavelli; the Englishman being a more systematic and philosophical thinker than his Florentine master, though a less acute and penetrating analyst of political experience. Hobbes, as is well known, accepted fully the Machiavellian view of human relations—outside the pale of a political society compacted through unquestioning obedience into peace and order. Outside this pale he certainly held any aggression or breach of compact conducive to self-preservation to be lawful to the human individual or group, struggling to maintain its existence in the anarchy called a state of nature; but he justified this licence on the ground that a member of such a "natural society" who may observe moral rules can have no reasonable expectation of reciprocal observance on the part of others, and must therefore merely "make himself a prey to others." In Hobbes' view, morality—the sum of the conditions of harmonious human living in society—is a system that man is always bound to keep before his mind as an ideal; but his obligation to realize it in act is conditional on a reasonable expectation of reciprocity. This condition is, I think, with careful limitations and qualifications, sound; and the error of Hobbes does not lie so much in making this demand for reciprocity—though he makes it too unguardedly—as in his palpable exaggeration of the difference between human relations in a so-called "natural" society and in the state of political order. The exaggeration is palpable—since (e.g.) the mere fact that the habit of making compacts prevails among states is evidence of a prevalent confidence that they will be more or less observed—but the exaggeration should not blind us to the real divergence that exists between the rules of public and of private duty, or to its connection with the cause that Hobbes assigns for it.

This divergence, observe, does not arise in the main from any fundamental difference in the general principles of ideal morality for states and individuals respectively, but from the actual difference of their relations. A similar, if not an equal, divergence would exist for a virtuous individual who found himself in a society where, whether from anarchy or from other causes, the moral standard maintained in ordinary conduct was as low as the moral standard of international conduct actually is.

As Mr. Spencer★ forcibly says—

> Ideal conduct . . . is not possible for the ideal man in the midst of men otherwise constituted. An absolutely just or perfectly sympathetic

★ *Principles of Ethics,* Part I., chap. xv., p. 280.

person, could not live and act according to his nature in a tribe of cannibals. Among people who are treacherous and utterly without scruple, entire truthfulness and openness must bring ruin. If all around recognize only the law of the strongest, one whose nature will not allow him to inflict pain on others, must go to the wall. There requires a certain congruity between the conduct of each member of a society and others' conduct. A mode of action entirely alien to the prevailing modes of action, cannot be successfully persisted in—must eventuate in death to itself, or posterity, or both.

I do not mean that the customary conduct of nations to each other is accurately represented by Spencer's description; but it is liable to resemble this description much more closely than the customary conduct of individuals in a civilized society. Nor, again, do I mean that a state, any more than an individual, can justify conduct which ideal morality condemns by simply alleging the similar conduct of other states—even the majority of other states: if this were so, moral progress would be almost impossible in international relations. From the fact that unprovoked aggression, committed with impunity and successful in its immediate aims, is a phenomenon that continually recurs throughout modern European history, I do not infer that it is right for a modern European state to commit an act of unprovoked aggression; what I contend is that this fact materially alters the moral relations between states by extending the rights and duties of self-protection.

The difference thus introduced is unmistakably, though vaguely, recognized in ordinary moral thought; all we have to do—according to the plan of the present essay—is to bring it clearly before our minds, and assign its limits as precisely as we can. Thus it has long been tacitly recognized that in international relations the conditions are wanting under which the morality of passive submission and resignation, specially distinctive of Christianity, is conducive to the general well-being. It has been comprehended by the common sense of the Christian world that the precept to turn the other cheek, and repay coercion and encroachment with spontaneous further concessions, was not given to nations; and that the meek who are to inherit the earth must be understood to be meek individuals, protected by a vigorous government from the disastrous consequences to themselves that meekness in a state of anarchy would entail.

The case is different with the rules of veracity, good faith, abstinence from aggression on person or property, which are not specially Christian: it would be absurd to interpret popular morality as allowing governments a general licence to dispense themselves from the obligation of these rules when they find it convenient, in view of the general tendency to transgress them. But to an important extent, in special cases, such a licence is commonly conceded. Take the case of veracity. We should not condemn a general in war for disseminating false statements to mislead the enemy, or for sending spies to obtain information as to the enemy's movements by processes involving an indefinite amount of falsehood. A similar licence is commonly conceded to governments—or at least to their subordinates—in performing the task of maintaining order within the community governed. We recognize that in the ceaseless contest with secret crime, the business of the detective police—which involves continual deception—is practically indispensable; and must therefore be regarded as a legitimate, if not highly honourable, calling. There is at present no such general toleration of the use of falsehood and spies and stratagems in diplomacy; times are changed, I am told, since the definition of a diplomatist as a person "sent to lie abroad for the benefit of his country," was from a scientific point of view admissible. But here again, I think, a reasonable expectation of reciprocity is practically accepted as a condition of the stringency of the rule prohibiting such artifices—a plot would be held to justify a counterplot, at any rate if there were no other effective means of defeating it.

In the case of breach of engagements, the extension of the scope of self-protection is of a somewhat different character. Our common morality does not justify treacherous promises, made without intention of fulfilling them, even in dealing with states that have been guilty of such treachery. Speaking broadly, the right mode of dealing with such a state is clearly to treat its promises as idle words, unless there is some adequate ground, other than the promise itself, for expecting its fulfilment. But when modern states have failed to carry out their compacts—and history abounds in instances of such failure—they have usually made excuses, alleging ambiguity of terms, material change of circumstances, or the non-fulfilment of promises on the other side. Now, in dealing with a government which—in order to free itself from inconvenient treaty-obligations—is in the habit of using pleas of this kind in a strained and unreasonable manner, I conceive that any other government would not be liable to censure for claiming a similar freedom—at any rate, in case of urgent need.

It will be observed that, according to the moral view that I am endeavouring to express, urgent need is held to be required—as well as the antecedence of similar acts on the other side—in order completely to justify a breach of veracity or good faith. Without urgent need, the fact that any particular act of unveracity or bad faith is merely imitative and retaliatory affords an excuse, but not an adequate justification; since even a retaliatory act of this kind has the mischievous effect of a bad precedent, and tends to depress the customary standard of morality between nations.

I may here mention one special difference between public and private morality arising from the same absence of a common government which has hitherto rendered wars between nations inevitable,—the different view that is and must be taken of the bindingness of compacts imposed by force in the two cases. In an orderly state, a promise obtained from any person by unlawful force has, of course, no legal validity: and it is at least doubtful whether it has any moral validity. If in England a robber were to force me, under threat of death, to promise him a large sum of money, I conceive that no thoughtful person would censure me for breaking my promise, though he might feel a sentimental preference for the opposite course. But in the case of states, we cannot similarly treat wrongful force as invalidating obligations deliberately undertaken under its pressure: to do this—as I have elsewhere said—"would obviously tend to aggravate the evils of unjust victory" in war: "as the unjust victor, being unable to rely on the promises of the vanquished community, would be impelled by self-interest to crush it utterly." At the same time, there is an opposite danger in treating oppressive conditions thus imposed as finally and permanently binding: as this would increase the temptation—already sufficiently strong—to skilfully-timed acts of violent aggression. In this dilemma, international morality has, I think, to adopt a somewhat vague compromise, and to regard such obligation as having a limited validity, but tending to lose their force through lapse of time, and the change of circumstances that lapse of time brings with it.★

So far I have been speaking of international relations; but the general

---

★ This general view may be made a little less vague by distinguishing different kinds of conditions imposed by unjust force. See my *Element of Politics*, chap. xvi., p. 6.

principles that I have applied to them must, I think, be admitted to some extent in respect of internal crises in the life of a political society. Here, however, I must guard against a misunderstanding. I do not think we should assume that the changes—even the greater changes—in internal polity, which the future has doubtless in store for European states, must necessarily involve violent breaches of political order, in respect of which the ordinary rules of morality are to be suspended. Revolutions and *coups d'état* are fraught with such wide and far-reached mischief that the efforts to avoid them should never be relaxed: if political meteorologists unite in affirming that one or other must come "sooner or later," the true patriot should answer, with Canning, that he "prefers it later." The same is, of course, true of wars: but there is at present more reason to hope for the ultimate success of such efforts in the case of internal strife owing to the greater strength of the bonds of interest and sympathy that unite members of the same state. But if ever such efforts seem doomed to fail, and the minds of men are turning to the violent courses that appear inevitable, an enlargement of the right of self-protection—somewhat similar to that which we have just recognized in international relations—must be conceded to any of the sections into which the state is suffering a transient moral disintegration; or rather to the statesmen acting on behalf of such a section.

The last sentence leads me to notice a reason sometimes given for divergence between public and private morality, which I have not yet considered. It is said that the actions of states have generally to be judged as actions of governments; and that governments hold a position analogous to that of trustees in relation to the community governed, and therefore cannot legitimately incur risks which a high morality would require individuals to incur in similar cases. I think that there is some force in the argument, but that it is only applicable within a very narrow range. Trustees, whether for private or collective interests, are bound to be just; and the cases are at any rate very rare in which the highest morality applicable in the actual condition of international relations would really require states to be generous at the definite sacrifice of their interests. For a state to embark on a career of international knight-errantry would, generally speaking, be hardly more conducive to the interests of the civilized world than to those of the supposed Quixotic community. Still I admit that cases may occur in which intervention of this kind, at a cost or risk to the intervening community beyond what strict self-regard could justify, would be clearly advantageous to the world, and that in such cases the "quasi-trusteeship" attaching to the position of government might render its duty doubtful. It would seem that in a case of this kind the moral responsibility for public conduct is properly transferred in a large measure from the rulers to the ruled. The government may legitimately judge that it is right to run a risk with the support of public opinion which it would be wrong to run without it; so that it becomes the duty of private persons—in proportion as they contribute to the formation of public opinion—to manifest a readiness to give the required support.

To sum up briefly the main result of a long discussion. So far as the past conduct of any foreign state shows that reciprocal fulfilment of international duty—as commonly recognized—cannot reasonably be expected from it, I admit that any other state that may have to deal with it must be allowed a corresponding extension of the right of self-protection, in the interest of humanity at large no less than in its own interest. It must be allowed to anticipate attack which it has reasonable grounds for regarding as imminent, to meet wiles with wiles as well as force with force, and to be circumspect in the fulfilment of any compact it may make with such a state. But I do not regard this as constituting a fundamental difference between public and private morality; similar rights may have to be exceptionally claimed and exercised between man and man in the most orderly society that we have experience of; the difference is mainly in the degree of exceptionality of the claim. It remains true that in both cases equally it must be insisted that the interest of the part is to be pursued only in such manner and degree as is compatible with the interests of the larger community of which it is a part; and that any violation of the rules of mutual behaviour actually established in the common interests of this community, so far as it is merely justified by its conduciveness to the sectional interest of a particular group of human beings, must receive unhesitating and unsparing censure.

IV

THE MORALITY OF STRIFE

ALL who have thought earnestly on moral questions, and in particular have reflected on the causes of and the remedies for the failure
to do what is right in themselves and others, must have recognized that
the causes of this failure divide themselves naturally under two distinct
heads. Firstly, men do not *see* their duty with sufficient clearness; secondly,
they do not *feel* the obligation to do it with sufficient force. But there are
great differences of opinion among thoughtful persons as to the relative
importance of these different sources of wrong conduct. The commonest
opinion is disposed to lay most stress on the latter, the defect of feeling or
will, and even to consider the defect of intellectual insight as having comparatively little practical importance. It is not uncommon to hear it said
by preachers and moralizers that we all *know* our duty quite sufficiently
for practical purposes, if we could only spur or brace our wills into steady
action in accordance with our convictions. And it is no doubt true
that, if we suppose all our intellectual errors and limitations to remain

An address delivered to the London Ethical Society in the year 1890.

unchanged, and only the feebleness of character which prevents our acting on our convictions removed, an immense improvement would take place in many departments of human life. But it is important not to overlook other inevitable results of the supposed change, which would certainly not be improvements. We all recognize the dangers of fanaticism. But what is a fanatic? Surely we all mean by a "fanatic" a person who acts up to his convictions, resolutely and perhaps vehemently, when they are opposed to the common sense of mankind, and when—in the judgment of common sense—his acts are likely to lead to gravely mischievous consequences. If, therefore, we suppose that the element of intellectual error in the causes of wrong action remains unchanged, while the element of feebleness of character, weakness of motive or will to do duty, is entirely removed, we must suppose fanaticism greatly increased. We must also suppose an increase in the bad effects of more widespread errors in popular morality, which are now often prevented from causing the full evil which they tend to cause, by the actual feebleness of the mistaken resistance which they oppose to healthy natural impulses. Hence, when we had to strike the balance of gain and loss to human happiness resulting from the change—though I have no doubt that the gain on the whole would be great—we must recognize that the drawbacks would be serious and substantial.

Considerations of this kind have led some thoughtful minds to take an exactly opposite view, and to regard it of paramount importance to remove the intellectual source of error in conduct, holding with Socrates that the true good of each individual man is really consistent and harmonious with the true good of all the rest; and that what every man really wants is his own true good, if he only knew it. But this view also is too simple and unqualified; since, in the first place, a man often sacrifices what he rightly regards as his true interest to the overmastering influence of appetite or resentment or ambition; and, secondly, if we measure human well-being by an ordinary mundane standard, and suppose men's feelings and wants unaltered, we must admit that the utmost intellectual enlightenment would not prevent the unrestrained pursuit of private interest from being, sometimes, anti-social, anarchical, and disorganizing. Still, allowing all this, it seems to me not only that a very substantial gain would result if we could remove from men's minds all errors of judgment as to right and wrong, good and evil, even if we left other causes of bad conduct unchanged; but that the gain in this case would be more unmixed than in the former case. Suppose, for instance, that every one who is liable to drink too much had clearly present to his mind, in the moment of temptation, the full amount of harm that his insobriety was doing to his bodily health, his reputation, his means of providing for those dependent on him; some, no doubt, would drink all the same, but the great majority of those not yet in bondage to the unnatural craving would draw back. Suppose, again, that any one who is wronging a neighbour saw, as clearly as any impartial judge or friend would see, the violation of right that he is committing; surely only a thoroughly bad man would persist in his wrong-doing. And thoroughly bad men are after all rare exceptions among the beings of mingled and chequered moral nature of whom the great mass of mankind consists, and who on the whole mean only to maintain their own rights and not to encroach upon the rights of others; though doubtless, from a mixture of intellectual muddle with passionate impulse or selfish negligence, they are continually liable to wrong others.

I have drawn attention to this fundamental distinction between (1) improvement in moral insight and (2) improvement in feeling and will, because I think it important that we should have a clear view of its general character before we enter on the special discussion of the "Morality of Strife," which is the subject of the present paper. I ought perhaps to explain that in speaking of strife I shall have primarily and chiefly in view that most intense form of conflict which we call war, in which masses of civilized men elaborately try to destroy each other's lives and incidentally to take each other's property. This is the strife which, from its fundamental nature and inevitable incidents, causes the most intense and profound moral aversion and perplexity to the modern mind. At the same time it seems to me that the deepest problems presented by war, and the deepest principles to be applied in dealing with them, are applicable also to the milder conflicts and collisions that arise within the limits of an orderly and peaceful community, and especially to those struggles for wealth and power carried on by classes and parties within a state. Indeed, these latter—though conducted by the milder methods of debate and vote—often resemble wars very strongly in the states of thought and feeling that they arouse, and also in some of the difficulties that they suggest.

Now, in considering the morality of strife, the difference of opinion which I have been discussing, as to the causes of wrong conduct in general, meets us with especial force. Thus many will say, when they hear of moralizing war, that the moralist ought not to acquiesce in its existence; he ought to trace it to its source, in the lack of kindly feeling among human beings. Spread kindness and goodwill; male altruism predominate over egoism; and wars between states will come to an end among civilized men, because there will be no hostile emotions to rouse them, while within states strife will resolve itself into a competition for the privilege of doing good to others. I do not deny that a solution of the problem of war for the world might be found in this diffusion of kindly feeling, if sufficiently ardent and universal. But for this effect the universality is necessary as well as the ardour. The increase of the "enthusiasm of humanity" in a moral minority, in a world where most men are still as selfish as now, would have no decisive tendency to prevent strife; for if around us some are wronging others, the predominance of altruism in ourselves, though it will diminish our disposition to fight in our own quarrels, will make us more eager to take part with others who are wronged; and since, so long as we are human beings, our kindly feelings must flow more strongly in special channels, as they grow in intensity we shall exhibit greater energy in defending against unjust attacks the narrower communities and groups in which we take special interest. Increase of sympathy among human beings may ultimately do away with strife; but it will only be after a long interval, during which the growth of sympathetic resentment against wrongs seems not unlikely to cause as much strife as the diminution of mere selfishness prevents. The Founder of Christianity is recorded to have said that he "came not to bring peace on earth, but a sword," and the subsequent history of Christianity offers ample and striking confirmation of the truth of the prediction. And the same may be said, with at least equal truth, of that ardour for the secular amelioration of mankind which we find presented to us in these latter days as a substitute for Christian feeling.

The extinction of strife through the extension of amity being thus at best a remote event, we may allow ourselves to dwell for a moment on the brighter aspects of the continuance of war. War is an evil; but it is not, from an ethical point of view, an unmixed evil. Indeed, its value as a school of manly virtue led the greatest thinkers of ancient Greece—even in the civilized fourth century—to regard the fighting part of the community as the only part on whose education it was worth while to bestow labour and care; the occupations of the trader and the artisan being considered an insuperable bar to the development of fine moral qualities. Christianity and the growth of free industry combined have carried European thought so far away from the point of view of Plato and Aristotle, that their utterances on this topic now seem to most of us startlingly narrow-minded and barbaric; but the element of truth that they contain still, from time to time, forces itself on the modern mind, and finds transient expression in a modified form. There are, I believe, even at the end of the nineteenth century, some thoughtful persons seriously concerned for moral excellence, who would regret the extinction of war; attracted not so much by the showy virtue of valour in battle, but by the unreserved devotion, the ardour of self-sacrifice for duty and the common good, which war tends to develop. If this acceptance of war as an indispensable school of virtue were widespread enough to impede the drift of modern opinion and sentiment towards universal peace as an ideal, it might be necessary to argue against it as a dangerous paradox. In such an argument we should not lay stress exclusively or even mainly on its physical mischief; but still more on its moral evils, its barbarous inadequacy as a means of settling disputes of right, the frequent triumphs of injustice and their demoralizing consequences, the constant tendency of the bitter resentments and the intensification of national self-regard, which war brings with it, to overpower the sentiments of humanity, and confuse and obscure those of justice and good faith. But I need not labour these points; the evils of war are so keenly felt that the moralist may without danger allow himself to make the most of the opportunities of moral development that it affords.

What I rather wish now to point out is, that the moral benefits of war, such as they are, depend largely on the fact that war is not usually—as cynics imply—a mere collision of passions and cupidities; it is a conflict in which each side conceives itself to be contending on behalf of legitimate interests. In the wars I have known, as a contemporary, this has been strikingly manifested in the sincere belief of religious persons generally—ordinary plain honest Christians on either side—that God would defend their cause. In the wars of ancient history a people's belief in special divine protection was not equally an evidence of its belief in the justice of its cause, since each nation had its own deities who were expected to take sides with their worshippers; but in a war between modern Christian nations, worshipping the same God, the favour of heaven implies the justice of the cause favoured; and it is sometimes startling to see that not only is each side convinced of its overwhelming claims to the favour of heaven, but it can hardly believe in a similar sincere conviction on the other side. Perhaps some of my readers may remember how, in the Franco-German war of 1870, the pious utterances of the Emperor William excited the derision of Frenchmen and their friends; it seemed to the latter not only evident that the invading Germans were brigands, but even impossible to conceive that they did not know that they were brigands. This strikingly shows how war among human beings, supposing them to possess the degree of rationality that average civilized humanity has at present reached, is normally not a mere conflict of interests, but also a conflict of opposing views of right and justice.

I must not exaggerate. I do not mean that in modern times unscrupulous statesmen have never made wars that were substantially acts of conscious brigandage, and have never been applauded for so doing by the nations whom they led, who have suffered a temporary obscurity of their moral sense under the influence of national ambition. I do not say that this has not occurred; but I do not think it is the normal case, and I shall leave it out of account, partly because it does not seem to me to give rise to any moral problem which we can profitably discuss. The immorality of such unscrupulous aggression is simple; and the duty is no less clear for any individual in the aggressing country to use any moral and intellectual influence he may possess—facing unpopularity—to prevent the immoral act. It may be difficult to say exactly how far he should go in such opposition; but the answer to this question depends so much on circumstances that an abstract discussion of it is hardly profitable.

It is still more true that in any strife of parties and classes within a modern civilized state, when there is a conflict of interests, it is not of bare interests, but of interests clothed in the garb of rights—and in the main the garb is not hypocritically worn. In such a state the sentiment of fellow-citizenship, the habit of co-operating for common ends, the community of hopes and fears stirred by the vicissitudes of national prosperity, tend powerfully to reinforce the wider sentiments of humanity and justice to men as men. Hence, though the predatory type of human being cannot be said to be rare in any civilized society, it is still an exceptional type; the average member of such a society is too moral to enter into a struggle on behalf of interests which he knows to be "sinister interests"—to use Bentham's apt phrase. I do not say that he is not easily led to believe that what is conducive to his interests is just—men's proneness to such belief is proverbial—but the belief is generally sincere; and though, again, in the heat of party conflict many things are done from passion and eagerness to win which are known to be wrong, these are deplorable incidents of party strife, they do not make up its moral texture.

If, then, normal human strife is due not merely to colliding interests, but to conflicting views of rights, it would seem that we might hope to reduce its worst effects to a sporadic and occasional evil, if we could only find and make clear the true definition of the rights in question. For though the interests of all individuals, classes, and nations are not harmonious, their rights are; that is the essential difference between the two. You cannot be sure of bringing disputants into harmony and peace by enlightening them as to their true interests, though you may in some cases; but you must do this if you can really and completely enlighten them as to their true rights, unless they are bad enough to fight on in conscious wrongful aggression. Such completeness of enlightenment, however, we cannot reasonably expect to attain; the complexity of human relations, and the imperfection of our intellectual methods of dealing with them, preclude the hope that we can ever solve a problem of rights with the demonstrative clearness and certainty with which we can solve a problem of mathematics. The practical question therefore is, how we can attain a tolerable approximation to such a solution.

To many the answer to this question seems simple. They propose to settle the disputes of right between nations, and the disputes of right between classes and sections within any state, by applying what I will call an *external* method; i.e., by referring the dispute to the judgment of impartial—and, if possible, skilled—outsiders, as the legal disputes of individual members of a civilized community are referred to arbitrators, judges, and juries. I call this an external method, because it does not require any effect to be produced on the intellects and consciences of the disputants; they are allowed to remain in their onesided and erroneous convictions; indeed, they are almost inevitably left to concentrate their attention on their own onesided views, and—if I may so say—harden themselves in their onesidedness, because their function in the process of settlement is to advocate their own case before the outside arbiter; they are not supposed to be convinced by his decision, but merely to accept it for the sake of peace.

The method takes various forms, according to circumstances. In the case of disputes between nations it takes the form of a substitution of arbitration for war; the practical—or, perhaps I may say, the technical—problem comes to be how to get a wise and impartial court of international arbitration. A similar method is widely advocated for the settlement of those disputes between employers and employed—within the limits drawn by the existing law—which have been so long a prominent feature of our present industrial condition. But in the still deeper disputes between classes and sections within a community, which tend to changes in the established legal order, the expedient commonly recommended is somewhat different; it consists in the construction of a legislature on the representative system, so adjusted and balanced that each class and section has enough representatives to advocate its claims, but not enough to constitute it a judge in its own cause; the decision on any proposed change in laws or taxation, affecting the interests of different sections in opposite ways, is always to rest with the presumably impartial representatives of other sections. Now, I do not wish to undervalue the external method in any of these cases; I think the attention of statesmen should be seriously directed to making it as perfect as possible. But I cannot believe that it is in any case safe to rely on it for a complete and final removal of the evils of strife.

Let us place ourselves at the point of view of a nation that is being drawn into what it regards as a just war, according to the received principles of international justice. It is obvious that any serious and unprovoked violation of international duty must be held to give a state whose rights are violated a claim for reparation; and if reparation be obstinately refused, it would seem that—so long as states are independent—the offending state must be held to have a right to obtain it by force, with the aid of any other states that can be persuaded to join it. This exercise of force need not necessarily amount to war. For instance, if the property belonging to a state or any of its members has been unjustly seized by another state, reparation may be obtained by reprisals; but it is most probable that such reprisals, being resisted, will lead to the thorough-going appeal to physical force as a means of settlement, which we call war. Well, at this point it is asked, by many earnest philanthropists, "Why should not the offended state make a proposal to submit its claims to arbitration, and why should not the offending state be made, by the pressure of public opinion, to accept this proposal?" I am far from waiving this suggestion aside as out of the range of practical politics. Much may be hoped, in the way of reduction of the danger of war between civilized states, from improvements in the machinery of arbitration, and a more extensive adoption of the improved machinery; and the efforts of those who keep urging these points on the attention of statesmen and of the public deserve our warmest sympathy. But I think that such efforts are more likely to attain the limited success which can alone be reasonably hoped, if those who urge them bear in mind the inevitable limitations of the applicability of arbitration to the disputes of right between nations.

In the first place, the violation of right which leads to a conflict may be a continuing evil, which requires immediate abatement as well as reparation; and the violence required for this abatement is likely to lead to further violence on the other side, so that the conflicting states may be drawn into the condition of war by a series of steps too rapid to allow of the delay necessary for arbitration, and which involve so many fresh grounds of complaint that the decision of the original dispute may easily sink into insignificance. But there are other reasons of more importance and wider application. On the one hand, the interests at stake may be so serious that a state, believing itself able to obtain redress by its own strong hand, cannot reasonably be expected to run the risk of arbitration, unless it can feel tolerably secure of impartiality in the arbitrator; or, to keep closer to the moral problem actually presented, I should rather say that the government of a community cannot feel justified in thus risking the interests of the community intrusted to it. On the other hand, where the quarrel is one that involves a conflict of principles, widely extended among civilized states, there may be an insuperable difficulty in finding an arbiter on whose impartiality both sides could rely. A similar difficulty may be caused by the ties of interest and alliance binding nations into groups. Thus, in the sixteenth and seventeenth centuries it would have been almost impossible to find such an arbiter in Europe in any quarrel between a Catholic and a Protestant state. In the nineteenth century it would be almost impossible to find such an arbiter in any quarrel caused by the claims of a nationality struggling for independence; while in the intervening period the combinations of states—formed, to a great extent, for the legitimate end of maintaining the "balance of power"—presented a similar obstacle.

Now, I think that history shows that minor violations of international rights—such as arbitration undoubtedly might settle—have rarely been the real *causes,* though they have often been the ostensible causes and the real *occasions,* of momentous wars. The most serious wars of the European group of states have resulted from conflicting fundamental principles, religious or political, or conflicting national interests of great real or supposed importance, or more often a combination of the two. Hence, though the international law which arbitrators can administer may be most useful in removing minor occasions of controversy and in minimizing the mischief resulting from graver conflicts, we can hardly look to it to provide such a settlement for the graver controversies as will enable us to dispense with war. This will perhaps appear more clearly if we reflect for a moment on the special difficulties that beset the definition of international rights, in consequence of which opposite views of imperfectly-defined rights tend to be combined with discordant interests. Such difficulties arise partly from the absence of a central government of the community of nations; partly from the imperfect unity and cohesion of a nation as compared with individual human beings; partly from the great difference in degrees of civilization in the society of nations; and practically we have also to take into account the comparatively small number of civilized states, and the consequent greater importance of an individual nation—and still more of a group of allied nations—relatively to the whole community whose affairs international law is designed to regulate. The first of these causes renders necessary and legitimate an extension of the right and duty of self-defence, which it is very difficult to limit. War is not only obviously just against actual aggression, but when aggression is unmistakably being prepared, the nation threatened cannot be condemned for striking the first blow, if this is an important gain for self-defence. But this easily passes over into anticipation of a blow that is merely feared, *not* really threatened. Indeed, this enlarged right of self-protection against mere danger has often been further extended to justify hostile interference to prevent a neighbour growing strong merely through expansion or coalescence with other states. I think that moral opinion should set itself steadily against this latter extension of the right of self-protection; still, it is obviously difficult to define exactly the degree of alarm that would justify hostile action. It is still more difficult to decide, on any clearly just principles, how far the right of national self-preservation may be legitimately extended into the right to prevent interference with "national development"—e.g., if nation A appropriates territory over which nation B is hoping to extend its sway some time or other. At the same time, this is a cause of strife that we must, I think, expect to operate more intensely as the world gets fuller. With each successive generation the demand for expansion on the part of civilized nations is likely to grow stronger; and the more serious the interests involved, the more difficult it will be to obtain acquiescence in the rules determining the legitimate occupation of new territory, which must inevitably be to some extent arbitrary. And the question is complicated by the differences in grade of civilization, to which I have referred; for the nations most advanced in civilization have a tendency—the legitimacy of which cannot be broadly and entirely disputed—to absorb semicivilized states in their neighbourhood, as in the expansion of England and Russia in Asia, and of France in Africa. As, I say, the tendency cannot be altogether condemned, since it often seems clearly a gain to the world on the whole that the absorption should take place; still it is obviously difficult to define the conditions under which this is legitimate, and the civilized nation engaged in this process of absorption cannot be surprised that other civilized nations think that they have a right to interfere and prevent the aggression.

When we turn to the part of the earth tolerably filled with civilized nations—to Western Europe—it seems that the duty of avoiding substantial encroachment would be so clear that it could not be violated without manifest immorality, if only such nations had perfect internal unity and coherence. I do not see, e.g., how any quarrel could easily arise between France and Spain—apart from collisions of interest in other parts of the world—except of the minor kind which arbitration might settle, unless there was something like avowed brigandage on one side or the other. But we have only to look at Germany and Italy to see that even Western Europe is far from being composed of states of this type; and even if internal unity were attained for a time, it might always be broken up again by some new division.

I therefore think it inevitable that, at least for a long time to come, every nation in the most important matters—as individuals in matters not within the range of law courts—must to an important extent be judge in its own cause; it may refer some of its disputes to arbitration—and I hope the number may increase—but there are others which it cannot so refer, and its judgment must determine the limits of such reference. Other considerations might be adduced, tending to restrict still further the normal application of arbitration in international controversies; e.g., it might be shown that even where both sides in such a controversy are animated by an adequate and preponderant desire for peace, an acceptable compromise is often more likely to be attained by direct negotiation than by reference to an arbitrator. But it belongs to a political rather than an ethical discussion to dwell on points like these. I have said enough to show why even civilized nations, in which the majority are so far moral as to be sincerely unwilling to fight for a cause clearly known to be wrong, cannot be expected to avoid war by arbitration, except to a very limited extent.

If, then, a moral acquiescence in war is at present inevitable, what is to be the aim of morality with regard to it? Chiefly, it would seem, twofold: to reduce its causes by cultivating a spirit of justice, and to minimize its mischievous effects by the prevalence of a spirit of humanity. Now in this latter point the progress of modern civilization shows a steady and considerable improvement,—though it must be admitted that the progress starts from a very low level. The growth of humane sentiment has established rule after rule of military practice, tending to limit the mischief of war to the *minimum* necessary for the attainment of its ends. Thus *bonâ-fide* non-combatants have been more and more completely exempted from personal injury, while as regards their property, the old indiscriminate pillage has given place to regulated requisitions and contributions, the severity of which at any rate falls short of cruelty. In the case of combatants, the use of instruments—such as explosive bullets—which tend to cause pain out of proportion to disablement has been expressly prohibited, and the old liberty of refusing quarter practically abandoned; while elaborate provision has been made for humane tending of sick and wounded soldiers; and humane treatment of prisoners, even at considerable inconvenience to their captors, is decisively imposed by the opinion of the civilized world. Much, no doubt, might yet be done in the same direction; but considering the aims of war, and the deadly violence inevitable in its methods, I think that civilized humanity, at the end of the nineteenth century, may look with some complacency on the solid amount of improvement achieved.

The case is different when we turn to the other duty of cultivating a spirit of justice. We all admit that—as we must be judges in our own cause—we ought to endeavour to be just judges; but there is hardly any plain duty of great importance in which civilized men fail so palpably as in this. Doubtless the impartiality required is difficult; still, I am persuaded that even the imperfect beings who compose modern nations might perform with more success the judicial function—which, in a modern state under popular government, has become, in some degree, the business of every man—if national consciences could be roused to feel the nobility, and grapple practically and persistently with the difficulties of the task. At any rate, the thoughtful and moral part of every community might fit themselves for this judicial function with more care, and perform it under a sense of graver responsibility than is now the case. I am not urging that they should keep coldly aloof from patriotic sentiment; but at any rate before the struggle has actually commenced, when the cloud of discord that is to cover the sky is as yet no bigger than a man's hand, it is surely the imperative duty of all moral persons, according to their gifts and leisure, to make an earnest and systematic attempt to form an impartial view of the points at issue.

There are three stages in such an attempt, which are not always distinguished. First, we may endeavour to put ourselves in the opponent's place, carrying with us our own principles and views of right, and see whether, when we look at the opponent's case from the inside, there is not more to be said for it then appeared when we contemplated it from the outside. Secondly, if we have no doubt that our opponent is in the wrong, according to principles of right that we sincerely hold, we still have to ask ourselves whether we apply these principles not merely in claiming our rights, but also in practically determining the performance of our duties. For if there has been divergence between our actions and our principles, though it may not always be a reason for abandoning a present claim— for two wrongs do not make a right—it is an argument for mildness and for a spirit of compromise. And, thirdly, if there seems to us to be a real difference of principles, then comes the most difficult duty of endeavouring to place ourselves in an impartial position for contemplating the different sets of principles, and seeing if there is not an element of truth in the opponent's view which we have hitherto missed. It is hard to bring a man to this when once the complex collision of principles and interests has begun, and it is still harder to bring a nation to it; but it is a plain duty imposed on us by reason, and it is the most essential part of the internal method of aiding the transition from strife to concord, without which the perfecting of the machinery of arbitration does not seem to me likely to achieve very great results. Fortunately it is not, for practical needs, indispensable that the opposing views of justice should be completely harmonized; it is practically sufficient if the divergence be so far reduced by reciporcal admissions that the difference remaining may appear to both less important than the evils of war. Thus the effort at mutual comprehension, even if it does not lead to anything like agreement, may still avert strife. For, finally, one great argument for the strenuous use and advocacy of what I may distinguish as the spiritual method of avoiding the appeal to brute force in international disputes—the cultivation of a spirit of justice—is that it tends to promote the application of the external or political method. If we school ourselves to seek no more than is our due in any dispute, and to take pains to ascertain what this is, we shall be practically more willing to submit our claims to arbitration; and, further, if a keen interest in international justice spreads through civilized nations, confidence in arbitrators will tend to increase.

I pause to consider briefly the burning question of the strife between industrial classes that is an increasingly prominent feature of modern civilized society; the strife which, so far as physical violence is excluded by political order, is carried on between two groups of producers—ordinarily manual labourers and employers—by means of concerted refusals to exchange productive services except on terms fixed by one or other of the opposing groups. There is no kind of strife to which the application of the method of arbitration appears at first sight more reasonable, or is more commonly demanded; but there is none in which the nature of the case ordinarily presents greater obstacles to the satisfactory application of it. The difficulty here is not so much to find an arbitrator adequately free from bias as to find principles of distributive justice which the common sense of both the classes concerned accepts. This is a difficulty that seems to reach its maximum in the present state of society, which is distracted between two opposing ideals. According to the individualistic ideal, monopoly and combination would only exist to an insignificant extent, and every individual worker would obtain, through unlimited competition, the market value—representing the social utility—of the services rendered by him to society. On the other hand, so far as we can conceive a completely socialistic *régime* to exist at all, we must suppose that the remuneration allowed to different classes of producers—beyond the minimum which anyone could obtain from the state in return for the work which it would have to provide for him somehow—would be determined by some administrative organ of government, on principles laid down by the legislature. In neither case would there be an opening for the industrial strife that naturally occurs in our present intermediate system, in which the pursuit of self-interest is more and more prompting to combined instead of simply competitive action. In this system the problem of determining the just or equitable division of any product, between two or more groups of the persons who have produced it, only admits of a rough and, to a great extent, arbitrary solution. Compulsory arbitration in the disputes thus arising would involve serious risks in a fully-peopled state; for the rules to be applied by the arbitrator would in the last resort have to be determined by government; and a state that undertook to fix the terms of industrial bargains would be responsible for any want of employment that might result, and would therefore be in a logically weak position for refusing to provide employment on the terms thus laid down; while if it attempted any such provision, full-blown Socialism would be well in sight. And even voluntary arbitration is, under these conditions, only applicable when the two parties have been somehow brought to agreement as to the general rules by which any particular dispute should be decided; and the difficult problem is how to bring them to this agreement. Here again, therefore, the external method of composing strife requires the aid of the spiritual method. For the reason I have explained, to appeal to the sense of justice, strictly speaking, of the opposing parties would be rather ineffective rhetoric. But we may none the less endeavour to develop the elements from which the moral habit of justice springs—on the one hand, sympathy, and the readiness to imagine oneself in another's place and look at things from his point of view; and on the other hand, the intelligent apprehension of common interests. In this way we may hope to produce a disposition to compromise, adequate for practical needs, even when the adjustment thus attained can only be rough, and far removed from what either party regards as ideally equitable.

My limits do not allow me to discuss the larger questions raised by the

V

THE ETHICS OF RELIGIOUS CONFORMITY

I HAVE taken as the subject of my address today the "Ethics of Religious Conformity." What I wish to discuss is the duty which the persons who form the progressive—or, to use a neutral term, the deviating—element in a religious community owe to the rest of that community; the extent to which they ought to give expression and effect to their opinions within the community; and the point at which the higher interests of truth force them to the disruption of old ties and cherished associations. There can, I think, be little doubt that this is an ethical question of much importance. But it may reasonably be doubted whether it is one with which we are here called upon to concern ourselves. I will begin by trying to remove this doubt.

The aim of our Society is to be a moralizing agency, to assist "individual and social efforts after right living." Now, actually, in the world we live in, the great moralizing agencies are the Christian churches; and the

A lecture delivered to the West London Ethical Society, November 24, 1895, and published in the *International Journal of Ethics*, April, 1896.

most advanced thinker can hardly suppose that this will not continue to be the case for an indefinite time to come. If so, surely none can be more seriously concerned than members of an Ethical Society that the vast influence exercised by the churches on social morality should be as pure and elevating as possible.

It is true that our work proceeds on a different basis; our principles are that "the good life has a claim on us in virtue of its supreme worth to humanity," and "rests for its justification" simply "on the nature of man as a rational and social being." But, in the view of the wiser and more thoughtful teachers in the Christian churches, this is not a basis to be rejected, though it needs to be supplemented. I will mention one or two great names. The philosophy of Thomas Aquinas has been for centuries the dominant philosophy in the Church of Rome. In the Anglican Church, and beyond its limits in England, there is no representative of orthodox Christian morality who has gained more esteem than Joseph Butler. Yet no one can doubt that in the view of Aquinas and of Butler equally it was a matter of the highest importance to show how—putting aside the Christian revelation—a life of virtue (not saintly virtue, but ordinary human virtue) might be justified on a consideration of the nature of man as a rational and social being.

Accordingly, in our Cambridge Ethical Society—though this is not, any more than yours, founded on the basis of acceptance of traditional Christian dogma—we have always invited, and, I am glad to say, obtained the co-operation of persons of orthodox views. It may seem, however, that this unexclusive attitude is incompatible with your express principle that the good life "rests for its justification on no external authority, and no system of supernatural rewards and punishments"; but I venture to interpret this principle as opposed not to Christian doctrine, but to a superficial and unphilosophic form of such doctrine. For in a more profound and philosophical view divine authority is not conceived as external; it is the authority of that Universal Reason through community with which all knowledge, all truth, comes to human minds. So, again, the rewards of virtue and the penalties of vice to which Christianity looks forward in the future lives of individuals are not "supernatural," since the conditions under which, if at all, those lives will be lived are conditions forming part of one system of nature—a system deriving its unity from the One Mind which is its ground. I am far from imposing this as an authoritative interpretation of your formula, but I trust I am right in regarding it as an admissible interpretation; since it is in this view of the scope of your principles that I accepted the honour of being your President, and of addressing you here today.

For while I have always sympathized with the movement that has led to the formation of Ethical societies here and in America, I have always held that they ought to maintain—and I hope that they always will maintain—towards the churches an attitude of fraternal sympathy, without either conflict or competition. The work that the churches are doing, with their vast resources and traditional influence over men's minds, is work in the efficacy of which we must always be keenly interested; while any work that we may accomplish in our little measure, towards the realization of our avowed aims, is work which the thoughtful among them will equally desire to be well done—though, of course, in *their* view it cannot be by itself adequate for the guidance of life.

It is, then, in this spirit that I address myself to the subject that I have annnounced.

The student of history sees that hypocrisy and insincere conformity have always been a besetting vice of established or predominant religions; and a grave drawback to their moralizing influence after the first period of ardent struggle is over, and they have attained a stable position of power and influence over men's minds. Indeed, we may say that in the popular classification of professional failings, just as lying is the recognized vice of diplomatists, chicanery of lawyers, solemn quackery of physicians, so hypocrisy is noted as the temptation of priests and of laymen who make a profession of piety. And in most of these cases, on the margin of the vice, there is a region of doubt and difficulty for persons desiring to do what is right: it is not easy to say exactly how far a diplomatist may legitimately go in concealing state secrets, or a lawyer in using his professional skill to defeat justice. It is on this margin of doubt and difficulty, in the case of religious conformity, that I wish now to concentrate attention. With the vice of hypocrisy, so far as it is conscious and unmistakable, I am not concerned. The thorough-paced hypocrite—

> *Who never naming God except for gain,*
> *So never took that useful name in vain—*

we may leave to popular censure;—which is, perhaps, at the present time sufficiently active in reprobating him. It is the excusable hypocrisy, the well-meant pretence of belief—the region not of vice, but of error in judgment, if error there be—that I wish now to examine.

And here I may pause to note another aspect in which the question I am raising interests us as an Ethical society. I conceive that it is largely a sense of the value of the churches as moralizing agencies—as supplying both in their regular common worship and their weekly discourses, an assistance to individual and social efforts after right living—which leads men who do not really believe important doctrines formally adopted by their church to cling to it in spite of intellectual divergence; and even, perhaps, in some cases to hold office in it and preach in its pulpits. They feel that the teaching received by them in childhood from their church or under its guidance has made them better men than they would have been without it, and they wish their children to be brought up under similar beneficent influences. Without denying that there are good men and women outside the churches, they think that—making a broad and general comparison of the religious and the irreligious—the conditions and habits of life of the latter are, on the average, manifestly less favourable to morality than those of the former. They think, therefore, that separation from the church would be—from an ethical point of view—a greater evil than a more or less suppressed intellectual disagreement with some of the doctrines in the creeds that they allow themselves to appear to believe.

The question then is, How far are they right? I need hardly explain, after what I have already said, that I propose to treat this question merely from an ethical point of view, and not at all as a theological question. Doubtless, in an age like the period immediately following the Reformation—when Christians still believed almost universally that there was some one ecclesiastical organization and some one system of doctrines to which the divine favour was exclusively attached, but were profoundly disagreed as to which organization or system enjoyed this privilege—any but a theological treatment of these topics would naturally seem idle. The inquiry then could only be, what degree of variation from the true standard involved deadly error. Even now, it may be held by some, that if a man has the misfortune to hold erroneous opinions he ought to keep them to himself, and outwardly appear to believe what he does not believe, rather than aggravate his guilt by the open rejection of saving truth.

Or they may hold that such a heretic must do wrong, whatever he does; he is in the miserable dilemma of being inevitably either a hypocrite or a schismatic, and it is an unedifying exercise in casuistry to discuss which is worst. On the other hand, men may still believe vaguely that the favour of heaven rests in some mysterious and supernatural way on a particular religious community, even though they may be unable to accept its distinctive theological opinions; or, rather, though they may have renounced most of its dogmas, but not the one dogma that asserts the peculiar salvatory efficacy of its discipline. To minds in any of these attitudes I do not attempt to appeal. Indeed, the mere statement of these views—though I believe them to be actually and, perhaps, even widely held—suffices to show how opposed they are to the general movement of thought in the present age, among Protestants at least, both within and without the churches. On the whole, the recognition of the necessity of free inquiry, and the respect for conscientious difference of opinion, is now so general among thoughtful persons that I believe most educated Englishmen—whether orthodox or not—are prepared to regard my question as one to be determined on ethical principles common to all sects and schools.

It is necessary, however, to separate this question from another one, that in many minds blends with it and predominates over it. It is very difficult for men in any political or social discussion to keep the ideal quite distinct from the actual, and not sometimes to prescribe present conduct on grounds which would only be valid if a distant and dubious change of circumstances were really certain and imminent. It is peculiarly difficult to do this in discussing the conditions of religious union; for in theological matters an ardent believer, especially if his beliefs are self-chosen and not inherited, is peculiarly prone to think that the whole world is on the point of coming round to his opinions. And hence the religious persons who, by the divergence of their opinions from the orthodox standard of their church, have been practically led to consider the subject of this lecture, have often been firmly convinced that the limits of their church must necessarily be enlarged at least sufficiently to include themselves; and have rather considered the method of bringing about this enlargement, than what ought to be done until it is effected. But when we survey, impartially, the development of religious thought from the Reformation to the present time; when we observe how the diversity of beliefs throughout the Christian world has continually increased, the interval between the extremes widening, and the intermediate opinions, or shades of opinion, becoming more numerous; when we see how little the outward organization, symbols, and formulas of the different religious communities have been affected by the discoveries of science or the changes of philosophy, or the successive predominance of novel ideas, novel hopes and aspirations, in the political and social spheres;—we shall feel it presumptuous to prophesy that any revolution is now impending in the nature, extension, and mutual relations of the recognized creeds of Christendom, so great as to render a discussion like the present unnecessary.

Here, however, it may perhaps be said, "Granting the question to be still one of practical importance, it is not one of fresh interest; it is surely an old question which must have been raised and settled—so far as ethical discussion can settle it—long ago." My answer is that the change of thought to which I just now referred—the movement in the direction of wide toleration—materially alters the conditions of the question; for this movement at once introduces a new danger and imposes a new duty. On the one hand, there is a danger that the disposition to tolerate and respect even widely divergent opinions, when held with consistency, clearness, and sincerity, may degenerate into a disposition to think lightly of conscious inconsistency and insincerity, and so to tolerate the attitude of sitting loose to creeds. On the other hand, every step society takes towards complete civil and social equality of creeds really diminishes the old excuse for lax and insincere conformity. Further, though the toleration of which I have spoken has, like other drifts of current opinion and sentiment, baser and nobler elements, its best element consists of the growing predominance of the love of truth over mere partisanship in theological controversy, which leads to a comprehensive effort after mutual understanding among persons who hold conflicting opinions. As a result of this we find, among the best representative of orthodoxy, a temperate dogmatism which holds opinions firmly and earnestly, and yet is able to see how they look when viewed from the outside, and to divine by analogy how the opinions of others look when viewed from the inside; and this attitude carries with it a legitimate demand for respectful frankness on the part of their opponents.

And this demand is continually strengthened by the growing influence of positive science as an element of our highest intellectual culture. I do not refer to any effect which the progress of science may have had in modifying theological opinions; but rather to the necessity, which this progress lays with ever-increasing force on theologians, of accepting unreservedly the conditions of independent thought which in other departments are clearly seen to be essential to the very life of knowledge. This is a necessity of which the recognition is quite independent of any particular view of theological method or conclusions. It is sometimes said that we live in an age that rejects authority. The statement, thus unqualified, seems misleading; probably there never was a time when the number of beliefs held by each individual, undemonstrated and unverified by himself, was greater. But it is true that we are more and more disposed to accept only authority of a particular sort; the authority, namely, that is formed and maintained by the unconstrained agreement of individual thinkers, each of whom we believe to be seeking truth with single-mindedness and sincerity, and declaring what he has found with scrupulous veracity, and the greatest attainable exactness and precision. For this kind of authority the wonderful and steady progress of physical knowledge leads educated persons to entertain a continually increasing respect, accompanied by a corresponding distrust of any other kind of authority in matters intellectual. Now, from theologians of an earlier generation, it seemed hopeless to look for acceptance of the conditions under which alone the authority of a "consensus" of experts can be obtained; owing to the one-sided stress which they were accustomed to lay on the imbecility of the inquisitive intellect, the inadequacy of language to express profound mysteries, and the unedifying effect of truth upon an unprepared audience. It is because a change is taking place in this respect, because among the most orthodox theologians there are men imbued with the best qualities of the scientific spirit, because the tide of opinion is moving in this direction among earnestly religious Protestants of all shades, that the time seems to me opportune for a fresh discussion of my present subject. If we accept as a fact, which at any rate cannot be rapidly altered, that the divergence of religious beliefs, conscientiously entertained by educated persons, is great, is increasing, and shows no symptom of diminution; if we admit the principles of complete toleration and complete freedom of inquiry; if we also admit the growing demand of educated laymen, that when they are instructed on matters of the highest moment they should feel the same security which they feel on less important subjects, that their teacher is declaring to them truth precisely as it appears to him,—then surely the old question as to the nature and limits of the duty of religious conformity may reasonably be examined afresh in the light of these considerations.

Now I find two views—opposed to each other, but both somewhat widely spread—which stand in the way of a full and frank discussion of this question. It is said that the question is so simple that it is not worth while discussing it at any length; an honest man can easily settle it on the principles of ordinary morality. Again, it is said that the question is so difficult and complex, and the right solution of it dependent on so many varying conditions, that it had better be left entirely to the conscience of the individual, which can take account of his special nature and circumstances. The truth seems to me to lie between these two extremes. On the one hand, I do not think it very difficult to find the right general answer to the question; though at the same time I do not think that this—for the persons whom it practically most concerns—is quite a simple answer. I think it requires both impartial sympathy and careful distinctions to conceive and state it accurately. On the other hand, I think that the best general answer that we can obtain is not one that by itself gives decisive guidance to any individual: it leaves, and must leave, much to be variously determined by the divergent views and sentiments and varying circumstances of different individuals; but I think we ought to confine these variations—in determining the conduct to which moral approval is to be given—within somewhat narrower limits than those within which the practice of well-meaning persons actually ranges.

The argument of those who treat the question as a simple one may be briefly given thus. A church is an association of persons holding certain distinctive doctrines;—not necessarily theological doctrines, since the essential differences between one church and another may relate to questions of ritual or of ecclesiastical organization rather than to questions strictly theological, but in any case doctrines or beliefs of some kind. An individual belongs to a church because he holds these distinctive doctrines; or at any rate because he once held them, and his intellect has not yet decisively rejected any important part of them, though it may be in a state of doubt and suspense of judgment on some points. It would be generally granted that, so long as he remains merely doubtful and wavering, he is right in maintaining his old position. But—according to this view— as soon as he has made up his mind against any important doctrine explicitly adopted by his church, it is proper for him to withdraw. Or at any rate—for I do not wish to state the view in the most extreme form—this withdrawal is a clear duty in the case of any church which exacts, as a condition of admission to the privileges of membership, an express declaration of adhesion to certain doctrines selected as fundamental in the teaching of the church.

This view of the basis of religious association cannot, I think, be rejected as an inadmissible view: we cannot say that an individual does wrong in holding and acting on it. I should go further and say that it is the most natural and obvious view to take. But it would, I think, be a grave mistake to impose it as the only view ethically admissible.

First, the view clearly does not correspond to the actual facts,—the actual basis of common understanding on which a church, in modern society, holds together. It is not only that the members of such a body do not always withdraw when they have ceased to hold any of its fundamental doctrines; but it is not expected that they should withdraw: they violate no common understanding in not withdrawing.

And this is because feelings that every one must respect make it impossible for a man voluntarily to abandon a church as easily as he would withdraw from a scientific or philanthropic association. The ties that bind him to it are so much more intimate and sacred, that their severance is proportionally more painful. The close relations of kinship and friendship in which he may stand to individual members of the congregation present obstacles to severance which all, in practice, recognize, if not in theory; but even to the community itself, and its worship, he is still bound by the strong bands of hereditary affection, ancient habit, and, possibly, religious sympathies outliving doctrinal agreement. Let us grant that these considerations ought not to weigh against disagreement on essential points. The question remains, Who is to be the judge of essentiality? For it often happens—probably most often at the present day—that the point at issue, though selected as fundamental by the church, is not so regarded by the divergent individual: it may very likely appear to him to possess no religious importance whatsoever, and therefore to give him no personal motive for secession. A man who feels no impulse to leave a community, and sees no religious or moral gain in joining any other, can hardly be expected to excommunicate himself; others, sympathizing with his motives, shrink from excommunicating him; and thus "multitudinism"—as it has been called—creeps tacitly into churches whose bond of union is *prima facie* doctrinal. And the principle thus admitted receives a continually widening application, until from the mere fact that a man is a member of a religious body we can draw no inference whatever as to his beliefs, even in the case of a generally upright and conscientious man, and even though the body to which he professedly belongs has a perfectly definite and express basis of theological doctrine.

It may be said that this result, however, is not legitimate or desirable, but merely a concession to human weakness, inevitable perhaps in fact so long as men are weak, but to be firmly rejected in determining the moral ideal. The reason, in my opinion, for adopting an opposite view is that the service which religion undeniably renders to society lies primarily in its influence on the moral and social feelings, and that Multitudinism tends to keep this influence alive in many cases in which a strict Doctrinalism would tend to destroy it. If a man severs himself from the worship of his parents and the religious habits in which he has grown up he will, in many cases, form no new religious ties, or none of equal stability and force; and in consequence the influence of religion on his life will be liable to be impaired, and with it the influence of that higher morality which Christianity, in all our churches, powerfully supports and inspires; so that his life will in consequence be liable to become more selfish, frivolous, and worldly, even if he does not lapse into recognized immorality. I need hardly say that I do not regard this as an inevitable result of breaking away from an inherited creed and worship. I do not even say that it is to be expected in a majority of cases. Many are saved from it by devotion to a nonreligious ideal—to science or social progress; others by the bracing effect of onerous duties faithfully discharged; others by intense and elevating personal affections. But—though I have no means of estimating the proportion with any exactness—I am disposed to think that this moral decline is to be feared in a number of cases sufficient to constitute it a grave danger.

Here I would note, because it is apt to be overlooked, one moral advantage of membership of a church for ordinary men—which remains even when the authoritative creed of the church no longer seriously affects their belief as to the moral order of the world—namely, that it constrains them, gently but effectively, to a regular and solemn profession of a morality higher than their ordinary practice. This may sound a paradox, since the gap between Christian professions and Christian practice is one of the tritest themes of modern satire. And I quite admit that for men deliberately and contentedly false to their avowed standard of duty the express acceptance of this standard is no gain, but a loss: they merely add the evil of hypocrisy to the evil of vice or selfish worldliness. But the case is otherwise with the average well-meaning persons who are numerically most important; however much their practice may fall below their professions, it is higher than it would have been if they had not, by professions not consciously insincere, given their fellow-men the right to try it by the exacting standard of Christian duty.

I need not labour this point here, since surely a leading motive for the formation of ethical societies is the desire to gain, for oneself and for others, the moral support to be derived from sharing in the social expression of lofty ethical aims and interests.

For these reasons I think that in defining the moral obligation of church-membership it is right and wise to admit what I have called Multitudinism, and concede to it as much as can be conceded without violating the principles of Veracity and Fidelity to promises.

Now probably you would allow me, if I wished, to assume that the rules of Veracity and Fidelity to promises are rules to be obeyed at all costs; that the evils of violating them at all are graver than any trouble and disturbance and pain that may be caused by strict adhesion to them. But this is not exactly my own view, and I wish here to explain my position with perfect frankness and precision. My philosophical principles are on ethical questions utilitarian. I think that these and other virtues are only valuable as means to the end of human happiness, and when I examine the matters discussed for ages by casuists, I find exceptional cases in which I have to approve of unveracity. For instance, I should not hesitate to lie to a murderer in pursuit of his victim, nor—if I thought it prudent—to deceive a burglar as to the whereabouts of the family plate. And there have been ages of violent and inquisitorial religious persecution when it was excusable, though not admirable, in a heretic to keep his view of truth a secret doctrine, and simulate acceptance of the creed imposed by fire and sword. But in an age like the present, when even aggressive atheism has in England been found no bar to a political career and parliamentary success, the last shadow of this excuse for unveracity has vanished.

But again, I admit cases in which deception may legitimately be practised for the good of the person deceived. Under a physician's orders I should not hesitate to speak falsely to save an invalid from a dangerous shock. And I can imagine a high-minded thinker persuading himself that the mass of mankind are normally in a position somewhat analogous to that of such an invalid; that they require for their individual and social well-being to be comforted by hopes, and spurred and cured by terrors, that have no rational foundation. Well, in a community like that of Paraguay under the Jesuits, with an enlightened few monopolizing intellectual culture and a docile multitude giving implicit credence to their instruction, it might be possible—and for a man with such convictions it might conceivably be right—to support a fictitious theology for the good of the community by systematic falsehood. But in a society like our own, where every one reads and no one can be prevented from printing, where doubts and denials of the most sacred and time-honoured beliefs are proclaimed daily from house-tops and from hill-tops, the method of pious fraud is surely inapplicable. The secret must leak out; the net of philanthropic unveracity must be spread in the sight of the bird: the benevolent deceiver will find that he has demoralized his fellow-men, and contributed to shake the invaluable habits of truth-speaking and mutual confidence among them, without gaining the end for which he has made this great sacrifice. The better the man who sought to benefit his fellow men in this strange way the worse, on the whole, would be the result; indeed, one can hardly imagine a severer blow to the moral well-being of a community than that that element of it which was most earnestly seeking to promote morality should be chargeable with systematic unveracity and habitual violation of solemn pledges, and be unable to repel the charge.

I conclude, then, that while we should yield full sympathy and respect to the motives that prompt a man to cling to a religious community whose influence on himself and others he values, even though he has ceased to hold beliefs which the community has formally declared to be essential; and while we should concede broadly the legitimacy of such adhesion; still all such concessions must be firmly limited by the obligations of Veracity and Good Faith.

This conclusion, however, is somewhat vague and general. I will try to make it rather more definite—but much must always be left to the varying sentiments and judgments of individuals, and it is an important gain to get the principle clear. In illustrating its application, I will consider first the case of pledges expressly taken on admission to membership. Here I should understand my principle to mean that the obligation to fulfil any such pledge should be held as sacred as any other promise, but that as broad an interpretation as is fairly admissible should be put on the terms of the pledge. In determining this I hold it reasonable to be largely guided by common understanding. This is not always easy to ascertain, but if an individual is in doubt, any serious danger of bad faith may usually be avoided by making his position clear to others who do not hold his views. The important point is that he should neither betray the confidence reposed in him by others, nor give them fair reason for believing that he holds opinions which he does not hold.

I may make this clearer by taking a particular example; and I will select the case of the Church of England, both because it is practically for us the most important case, and because in an established church with a prescribed form of worship, and an elaborate official creed more than three centuries old, the difficulties of the present question reach their maximum. Now there can be no doubt that a member of the Church of England is formally pledged to believe the Apostles' Creed. But it is clearly impossible to take this pledge literally. If it comes into conflict with the necessity or duty of believing what appears to a man true, it can be no more binding than any other promise to do what is either impossible or wrong. Can we say, then, that in the case of such conflict there is an implied pledge to withdraw? This is, I think, the most natural view to take, and, for a long time, I thought it difficult to justify morally any other view. But as the pledge to withdraw is at any rate only implied, and as the common understanding, of orthodox and unorthodox alike, gives the implication no support, I now think it legitimate to regard the obvious though indirect import of the verbal pledge as relaxed by the common understanding. At the same time, considering how necessarily vague and uncertain this appeal to a tacit common understanding must be, and how explicit and solemn the pledge taken is, I do not think anyone who is a candidate for any educational or other post of trust, in which membership of the English Church is required as a condition, ought to take advantage of this relaxation without making his position clear to those who appoint to the post; so as to make sure that they, at any rate, are willing to admit his interpretation of it. I do not mean that such a person is bound to state his theological opinions—I think no one should be forced to do that—but I think he ought to state clearly how he interprets his pledge to believe the Apostles' Creed.

I might pursue this question into much more detail, but this kind of casuistry is apt to weary, unless it is pursued for the practical end of personal choice or friendly counsel; and I am anxious not to seem to dogmatize on points on which I should readily acquiesce in minor differences of judgment. I pass on, therefore, to examine the obligation implied in taking part in a form of worship—especially one which, like that of the Church of England, includes the recital of one or more creeds. Here, however, I think that the only practical question admitting of a precise general answer relates not to the duty of a private member of the church, but to the duty of its appointed teachers. For the mere presence at a religious service—by a clear common understanding—does not imply more than a general sympathy with its drift and aims; it does not necessarily imply a belief in any particular statement made in the course of it, as an ordinary member of the congregation is not obliged to join in any such statement unless he likes. And how far it is desirable that an individual should take any part in a social act of religious worship, while conscious of a certain amount of intellectual dissent from the beliefs implied in the utterances of the worship, is a question which may properly be left to be decided by the varying sentiments of individuals; the effect of public worship on the worshipper is so complex and so various, that it would be inexpedient to attempt to lay down a definite general rule. The minds of some are so constituted, that it would be a mockery to them to take part in a service not framed in exact accordance with their theological convictions; to others, again, quite as genuinely religious, but more influenced by sympathies and associations, the element of intellectual agreement appears less important.

The case of the teacher, the officiating minister, is different, for on him the imperative duty falls—in the Church of England—of solemnly declaring his personal belief in the fundamental doctrines of the church, as stated in the Apostles' Creed and the Nicene Creed. And here, I think, we come to a point at which the efforts made for more than a generation in England to liberalize the teaching of the English Church, and to open its ministry to men of modern ideas, must find an inexorable moral barrier in the obligations of veracity and good faith. For the priest who recites any one of the precise and weighty statements in the Apostles' Creed,★

★ I mention the Apostles' Creed because its position in the Baptismal Service attaches to it with special emphasis the character of a summary of the doctrine which the minister has been appointed to teach.

while not really believing it, can hardly be acquitted of breaking both these rules of duty;* since he states falsely that he believes a theological proposition which he has implicitly pledged himself to teach with genuine belief, and in his case no common understanding can, I think, be held to have relaxed the force of this pledge. I believe that there are men who make these false statements regularly with the best intentions, and with aims and purposes with which we shall all here sympathize; but the more we sympathize with them, the more it becomes our duty to urge—from the purely ethical point of view which we here take—that no gain in enlightenment and intelligence which the Anglican ministry may receive from the presence of such men can compensate for the damage done to moral habits, and the offence given to moral sentiments, by their example. Let me not be misunderstood. I should desire and think right that in determining the scope of the obligation imposed by the creeds the utmost breadth of interpretation should be granted, the utmost variety of meanings allowed which the usage of language, especially the vagueness of many fundamental notions, will fairly admit. Christianity, in the course of its history, has adapted itself to many philosophies; and I do not doubt that there is much essentially modern thought about the Universe, its End and Ground and moral order, which will bear to be thrown into the mould of these time-honoured creeds. But there is one line of thought which is not compatible with them, and that is the line of thought which, taught by modern science and modern historical criticism, concludes against the miraculous element of the gospel history, and in particular rejects the story of the miraculous birth of Jesus. I would give all sympathy to those who are trying to separate the ethical and religious element in their inherited creed from the doubts and difficulties that hang about the "thaumatological" element, and so to cherish the vital ties that connect the best and highest of our modern sentiments and beliefs, religious and moral, with the sacred books and venerable traditions of Christianity. I think the work on which they are engaged a good work and profitable for these times; but I cannot think it is a work that can properly be done within the pale of the Anglican ministry.

---

* No doubt if he at the same time makes clear that he does not believe the statement, his unveracity is merely formal; but then his breach of his ordination vow, "so to minister the doctrine . . . as this Church hath received the same," becomes still more palpable.

VI

CLERICAL VERACITY

IN January, 1897, a reply from the Rev. H. Rashdall of Hertford College, Oxford, combating at some length the view taken in my address as to the moral position of the Anglican clergy, appeared in the same journal. Mr. Rashdall's paper is ably and earnestly written, and I have endeavoured to give full weight to the considerations urged by him. But the main conclusions expressed in my address remain unchanged; and as the question seems to me one of profound social importance, I propose in this essay to return to it and give such further explanations and further arguments as Mr. Rashdall's paper suggests. I do not, however, find it convenient to throw my statement into the form of a simple rejoinder to Mr. Rashdall, because he has, to an important extent, misunderstood my position; and the detailed discussion of such misunderstandings is almost always wearisome and unprofitable to the reader. The misunderstanding is partly due to the comparative brevity with which I treated the subject—Mr. Rashdall's thirty pages being in fact directed against the last page and a half of my address; and

The above address was published in the *International Journal of Ethics* for April, 1896.

perhaps I ought to offer some explanation of this brevity. The truth is that though Mr. Rashdall regards my position as extreme on the side of strictness, "almost what might have been expected from a Kantian rigorist," this was not at all my own view of it. I do not merely mean that I aimed at keeping a judicious middle course, avoiding with equal care right-hand rigour and left-hand laxity; for that, I suppose, is the aim of every one who forms a disinterested conclusion on a controverted matter. The point is rather that, while composing my address, my "judicious mean" seemed to myself much more assailable in respect of laxity than in respect of rigour. Before writing it, I had tried to study impartially the Baptismal Service and the Confirmation Service of the Church of England; and had been strongly impressed with the definiteness and force with which the doctrinal basis of membership is there put forward. A member of the Church has been "baptized in the faith" defined by the Apostles' Creed; at confirmation he has solemnly "acknowledged" himself "bound to believe" it. I had, therefore, some hesitation in arguing, on the ground of anything so vague as a tacit common understanding, that a layman who definitely rejects any precise and important statement made in this creed may still legitimately claim the privileges of membership. I felt that if this claim were denied by any one of the many orthodox persons who regard the Apostles' Creed as the indispensable minimum of Christian doctrine, I should have considerable difficulty in defending the position that I had still, on the whole, determined to maintain. On the other hand, the proposition that an ordained minister of the Church, who is required by his office to declare solemnly every Sunday his belief in the Apostles' Creed, is chargeable with unveracity if this declaration is palpably false—this proposition seemed to me hardly controvertible. I was, indeed, aware that a portion of the Anglican clergy were in the habit of thus affirming falsely their belief in the miraculous birth of Jesus Christ; because Mr. Haweis, in an interesting article in the *Contemporary Review* (September, 1895) had stated this as a fact within his knowledge. "We have in our midst," said Mr. Haweis, "clergy within the Church holding two views of the incarnation. There are what I may call the prenatal infusion clergy and the postnatal transfusion clergy. The Postnatalists admit human parentage on both sides." I had no doubt that these Postnatalists*

---

* I propose in this article to adopt Mr. Haweis' term, as a convenient designation for "Christians who do not believe in the miraculous birth of Jesus Christ."

were for the most part making their weekly false statements with the best intentions; but it never occurred to me that they would claim to be acquitted of unveracity in so doing. I rather supposed them to hold that any harm that might be done to religion and morality by this falsity was outweighed by the loss that the Church would suffer if men of enlightenment, open to modern ideas and fearlessly accepting the methods of modern criticism, were excluded from its pulpits. This was a plea that I was prepared to discuss more fully if necessary; but on the point of veracity I thought I might be brief.

It is partly owing to this brevity that Mr. Rashdall has occupied a considerable part of his article with arguments really irrelevant to my position. Thus he argues at length against the view that a clergyman is bound to believe in miracles as such, and in all the miracles recorded in the New Testament. But I did not intend to suggest this; my contention was merely that veracity requires him to believe the marvels affirmed in the creeds. He is quite at liberty—so far as my argument is concerned—to hold that these marvels were "not breaches of natural law."

I cannot, however, admit that Mr. Rashdall's misunderstandings are entirely due to my brevity. For instance, he understands me to suggest that a clergyman is bound to believe "in the *most literal** interpretation of everything contained in the creeds." But in the paragraph against which he was arguing I had expressly said "I should desire and think right that in determining the scope of the obligation imposed by the creeds, *the utmost breadth of interpretation should be granted, the utmost variety of meanings allowed,* which the usage of language, especially the vagueness of many fundamental notions, will fairly admit." My contention is simply that the widest licence of variation that can be reasonably claimed must stop short of the permission to utter a hard, flat, unmistakable falsehood; and this is what a clergyman does who says solemnly—in the recital of the Apostles' Creed—"I believe in Jesus Christ, . . . who was conceived by the Holy Ghost, born of the Virgin Mary," when he really believes that Jesus was, like other human beings, the son of two human parents. He utters, of course, a similar falsehood in affirming the belief that Jesus "on the third day rose again from the dead," when he does not believe that Jesus had a continued life as an individual after death, and a life in some sense

---

* The italics are mine.

corporeal. But since the conception of the resurrection body—which, in a theology based on the canonical scriptures, is naturally formed by comparing the language of St. Paul (I Cor. xv.) with the language of the third and fourth evangelists—is somewhat ambiguous and obscure,* I propose in this discussion to concentrate attention mainly on the first-mentioned statement, which presents a perfectly simple and definite issue.

This issue is frankly accepted by Mr. Rashdall. He definitely holds that a man may reject the miraculous birth and yet solemnly recite in church the Apostles' Creed and the Nicene Creed, without doing anything "really inconsistent with the duties of veracity and good faith," according to the "principles which are generally recognized."

His reasoning is as follows:[†]

1. "The clergy do not profess their beliefs in the Creeds in any other sense and to any other degree than they assent to the whole of the Prayer Book and Articles."
2. There are few clergymen who literally believe all the Thirty-nine Articles; and even in the Apostles' and the Nicene Creed there are clauses which "most orthodox clergymen would explain in a way different from that which was intended by their authors"—e.g., those relating to the descent into hell, and the Resurrection of the Body.

---

* The difficulty in making the conception precise arises thus. St. Paul, expounding the distinction between the ψυχικὸν and the πνευματικὸν σῶμα, says that "flesh and blood cannot inherit the kingdom of God." But according to St. Luke the resurrection body of Jesus is seen to have "flesh and bones," and to eat fish and honeycomb; according to both St. Luke and St. John the risen Jesus offers His body to be handled; and it is clearly contrary to the meaning of the Evangelists to suppose these appearances and offers deceptive. On the other hand, the form of Jesus appears and vanishes mysteriously (Luke xxiv. 31, 36), and seems to have passed through closed doors. (John xx. 19, 26.)

I observe that Alford (on Luke xxiv. 39) suggests that the resurrection body had flesh and bones, *but not blood*. This strikingly illustrates what I have ventured to call the "obscurity and ambiguity" of the conception; but it is not easy to treat the suggestion with the respect due to a learned and thoughtful commentator. The declaration appended to the Anglican Communion Service, on the contrary, affirms that "the natural Body *and Blood* of our Saviour Christ are in heaven."

The scriptural data being what I have just stated, I think that a large freedom of interpretation of the term "body" may be legitimately claimed by any one who affirms a belief in the "resurrection of the body."

† In what follows I have endeavoured faithfully to represent Mr. Rashdall's arguments, keeping his own words as far as possible, but I have found it necessary for clearness to give them in a different order.

3. We have to recognize, accordingly, a "general agreement that subscription does not imply a literal acceptance of the formulæ."

4. The liberty thus gained might with advantage be increased; and, with a view to this increase, "the principle of liberalizing interpretation may be carried a little further than can be justified by strict insistence upon" the rule that "words must be taken to mean what they are generally understood to mean." By so doing a clergyman will "contribute to a further step in that process of religious development which has proved so beneficial in times past."

5. This principle justifies a clergyman in affirming his belief that Christ was born of a virgin, when he really believes that He had two human parents, provided he thinks the matter "of no spiritual significance."

6. No doubt such a man ought, before taking orders, to satisfy himself that this "disbelief is of the same order as those which public opinion has already recognized as falling within the permissible limits"; and Mr. Rashdall appears to concede that he may have some little difficulty in satisfying himself of this: but he thinks that he is "justified in throwing the responsibility" on the bishop to whom he applies for ordination. If the bishop consents to ordain him, as an avowed unbeliever in the miraculous birth, he may feel assured that his disbelief "does not exceed the limits of the liberty which the Church by its practical conduct has proclaimed." Nor need he—if I understand Mr. Rashdall—communicate to the world or to his congregation his unbelief in the miraculous birth. It is sufficient if he informs his bishop and the incumbent who gives him his title, and lets his congregation know "by the general tenor of his teaching" in what sense he interprets his acceptance of the formularies.

7. For confirmation of his general view of the liberty allowed to the clergy, Mr. Rashdall appeals to "the Courts, the authorized interpreters of the obligations imposed by law upon the clergy." He finds that the "decisions of the Judicial Committee of the Privy Council in the case of the various writers in *Essays and Reviews* go far to constitute, within the limits contended for in this article, a charter of theological freedom for the clergy of the Church of England."

This is, I think, a faithful summary of the reasoning by which Mr. Rashdall tries to prove that the conduct he recommends is "not really inconsistent with the duties of veracity and good faith." I cannot say that he has convinced me on either point; but after considering the line of his argument, I think it better to separate the duties of veracity and good faith, and, for clearness of issue, to concentrate attention here mainly on the former. The pledges given by a priest at his ordination are no doubt given immediately to the bishop; and it is at least a tenable view that the bishop is an authorized interpreter of the ordination vows "so to minister the doctrine as this Church hath received the same," and "with all faithful diligence to banish and drive away all strange doctrines contrary to God's Word." Hence the question, whether in the exercise of this interpretative authority he may properly dispense an enlightened candidate from the duty of believing and teaching such portions of the Apostles' Creed as conflict with modern historical criticism, may perhaps be regarded as a question of ecclesiastical order with which an outsider should not presume to deal. I should myself have thought that this episcopal dispensing power was rather a mediæval than a modern idea; but I do not claim to be an expert on such points. I will only say that if this dispensing power be once admitted, I do not see how it is possible to limit it to the particular modern ideas that Mr. Rashdall wishes to admit. Suppose, for instance, that a disciple of Matthew Arnold, glowing with ardour to exhibit the "true greatness of Christianity," purified from the "popular *Aberglaube*" of the Apostles' Creed and the "false science" of the Nicene Creed, presents himself for ordination before a bishop who—like the present Dean of Ripon*—is more or less in sympathy with *Literature and Dogma*. Is it not probable that the enlightened prelate would stretch his dispensing power to admit the enlightened candidate? and could a colleague who had himself consented to ordain a Postnatalist reasonably censure the transaction?† I can hardly think that the Church of England will ever willingly entrust such a power to any single bishop.

But in any case we shall agree that this episcopal dispensing power cannot extend to the general duty of veracity: the bishop cannot license a

---

* See *Fortnightly Review*, vol. xlviii, pp. 452–8.

† I do not know that any bishop has actually gone quite so far. Mr. Rashdall, indeed, informs us that "the most learned and universally respected theologican among the English bishops of this generation consented to ordain a candidate who confessed to him that the question of the miraculous birth was to him an open question." But there is a not immaterial difference between saying that one believes what one disbelieves, and saying that one believes something about which one is suspending one's judgment. Mr. Rashdall's bishop may have allowed himself to hope that the balance of his candidate's judgment would shortly incline on the orthodox side.

deacon or priest to speak falsely to his congregation. And here I must express my astonishment at Mr. Rashdall's assertion that the clergy do not profess their belief in the Creeds in any other sense or degree than they assent to the whole of the Prayer Book and the Thirty-nine Articles. For he himself points out that the assent required to the Prayer Book and Articles is only a "general declaration of assent, deliberately substituted by Parliament and both convocations in 1865 for certain very much stronger and more explicit declarations; so that in distinguishing between a general belief in the Articles and Prayer Book, and an explicit belief that everything in the Articles and Prayer Book is true, no one can be accused of pressing an accidental selection of phrases." But an "explicit belief that everything" in the Apostles' Creed "is true" is just what everyone who performs clerical functions has to declare; moreover, he has ordinarily to declare it every Sunday, whereas his general assent to the Articles is only required when he is ordained or licensed to a curacy, or instituted to a benefice. Mr. Rashdall's arguments to show that hardly any clergyman really believes everything in the Thirty-nine Articles would only be to the point if every clergyman were required periodically to repeat all the Articles, prefacing each with the words "I believe": under the conditions which have now existed for a generation such arguments are, by his own showing, irrelevant to the present issue.*

At the same time the considerations which Mr. Rashdall urges against a pedantic insistence on what he calls "technical veracity," in dealing with formulæ prescribed for assent or repetition, seem to me to a great extent sound. My complaint is that, instead of stating and applying these considerations with the care and delicacy of distinction required for helpfulness, so as to show how the essence of veracity may be realized under peculiar and somewhat perplexing conditions, he rather uses them to suggest the

* For this reason I have not thought it worth while to discuss Mr. Rashdall's *tu quoque,* addressed to the High Chruch party. I should admit that it would have had some force before 1865; but now any difficulty that a High Churchman may find in agreeing to the statements of any particular Article are *prima facie* met by the difference between general assent and explicit belief in particulars, on which Mr. Rashdall lays stress. It is possible, indeed, that the divergence between the opinions of some extreme High Chruchmen and the general scheme of doctrine set forth in the Articles may be too great to be fairly covered by this difference. But Mr. Rashdall has made no serious attempt to prove this; and it would be difficult to demonstrate it cogently, owing to the inevitable indefiniteness of the effect of the change made in 1865.

depressing and demoralizing conclusion that no clergyman can possibly speak the truth in the sense in which a plain layman understands truth-speaking; so that any clergyman may lie without scruple in the cause of religious progress, with a view to aiding popular education in the new theology, and still feel that he is as veracious as his profession allows him to be. Or perhaps I should rather say that Mr. Rashdall's conception of substantial veracity is what grammarians call *proleptic;* the duty of truth-speaking is, he thinks, adequately performed by a Postnatalist, if he may reasonably hope that the falsehood he now utters will before long cease to deceive through the spread of a common understanding that he does not mean what he says. In this way what is sound in Mr. Rashdall's arguments comes to be inextricably mixed up with what I regard as dangerously misleading. It appears to me therefore desirable that I should state and illustrate in my own way the general view of the moral obligation of veracity in which we on the whole agree, and then try to show that, properly understood, this does not support his particular conclusions as to clerical duty.

Two considerations appear to me to modify the duty of truth-speaking in such a case as that before us.

1. Ordinarily a man may choose his own words to express his belief, and therefore has no excuse for deliberately choosing ambiguous words; he ought, generally speaking,* to choose words which appear to him freest from ambiguity. But where the words are prescribed for him this choice is precluded; and in such a case, I conceive, he should be held to speak truthfully, if he employs the terms in any sense which they will fairly admit, according to the common usage of language. I think that this is the rule which a conscientious man practically applies in any of the cases—not rare in modern political life—in which he is asked to sign a document which he has had no share in drawing up. If it contains any statement as to a matter of fact which he regards as clearly false, he will refuse to sign the document, however much he may sympathize with its object; but he will sign it—in a good cause—although the document may contain some phrases which he can only accept by taking them in a sense

---

* I should hold that even when we choose our own words, there are cases in which regard for the feelings of others may properly lead us to prefer words to some extent ambiguous.

different from that which the majority attach to them, and perhaps different from that intended by the framers of the document, provided the vague and varying usage of common speech may be fairly held to include the different meanings. It is the common usage and understanding which fixes the limits of variation in such cases, not simply the opinions and sentiments of the framers of the document.

2. This leads us to the second consideration. The common understanding may change gradually, so that certain phrases in certain relations may come to be understood in a sense quite different from that which they originally bore, or which the words would convey if used in other connexions. The stock instance of this is the language of compliment or politeness: thus the phrase "Dear Sir" in commencing a letter is understood to express not affection, but a certain minimum of social respect; similarly the words "Right Reverend" might be applied without deception to a bishop by a Nonconformist, who both hated prelacy and despised the particular bishop to whom he was writing. In some cases the new meaning thus given to a phrase by current usage is designed to be ambiguous, because ambiguity is required by social convenience. Thus the phrase "not at home" is now understood to mean *"either* out *or* unwilling to receive visitors";—a phrase with this ambiguous meaning being convenient, because the uncertainty between the two alternatives tends to prevent social friction.

This last example has a peculiarity which deserves special attention from our present point of view. The meaning now attached to the phrase "not at home" is the result of a gradual process of change during which the phrase has been, in a continually decreasing degree, deceptive. Now the original deceptive use is obviously condemned by the general rule to truth-speaking, and few thoughtful persons would deny that it was morally objectionable: it was a falsehood not justified by the social convenience which prompted it. The question then arises whether this deception in the process of change—granting it wrong—renders it wrong to avail ourselves of the results of the process? I agree with Mr. Rashdall in thinking that this question must be answered in the negative. In the political and social life of man good continually comes out of evil, and bad actions have, as a part of their consequences, beneficent results,—as when a prosperous and well-ordered state has been founded by unscrupulous aggression and conquest. In all such cases we may, I conceive, use the results freely without approving the process.

A more subtle question, somewhat less easy to answer, arises in respect of the later stages of the process to which I have referred. The new meaning may be understood by a large number of the persons to whom the phrase is addressed, but not by all; there may still be a certain amount of deception caused by its use, and some of those who use it may be conscious of deceiving. Is it at this stage legitimate to use it? and, if so, at what point of the gradual process has it become legitimate? The general answer is, that it becomes legitimate when the evil of social annoyance which the phrase would prevent becomes less than the evil of deception; but in the case supposed the line cannot be drawn exactly, and the practical decision must be left entirely to the varying judgment of individuals. We shall find, however, that the corresponding problem is to some extent easier to solve in dealing with the more important matters with which this essay is concerned—to which I now return.

There can be little doubt that old prescribed expressions of religious belief do tend to have their meaning changed by changes in prevalent theological opinion; and in some cases the early stages of the process may have involved conscious deception,—of which, according to the rule just laid down, we shall disapprove, while at the same time allowing as legitimate the employment of the phrase in the new meaning, when the change in common understanding has been brought about. But it is by no means necessary that any conscious deception should take place, as the change of meaning may be so gradual that neither speaker nor hearer is at any time aware that he is using words in a non-natural sense. There seem to be two chief forms of this process: (1) Words originally used literally come to be used metaphorically, and (2) words originally intended to be understood without qualification come to be used with tacit qualifications and reserves, which materially modify their meaning.

Both these kinds of changes have certainly taken place in respect of the common understanding of the formulæ of the Church of England; and I should regard them both as legitimate, so long as the new meaning is one which the phrases in question will admit without any violent straining.

Let me give one or two examples. The Apostles' Creed makes the following assertions with regard to Jesus Christ:

"On the third day He rose again from the dead, He ascended into heaven, And sitteth on the right hand of God the Father Almighty; From thence He shall come to judge the quick and the dead."

It seems clear that the original meaning of these phrases is that unmistakably expressed in the Fourth Article: "Christ . . . took again His body, with flesh, bones, and all things appertaining to the perfection of man's nature; wherewith He ascended into heaven and there sitteth, until He returns to judge all men at the last day."

That is, the older belief clearly was that Jesus not only went from the earth upwards with "flesh, bones, etc.," but that He is now existing with these elements of bodily life in a certain portion of space called heaven. And the same view is no less definitely expressed in the declaration appended (for quite another purpose) to the Communion Service: "the natural body and blood of our Saviour Christ are in heaven, and not here; it being against the truth of Christ's natural body to be at one time in more places than one."

Now I think that this belief hardly survives at all in the minds of educated persons at the present time. At any rate among the educated laity I doubt if even the most orthodox—however firmly they believe that in the actual existence of Jesus Christ the spiritual union of human and divine natures is perpetually maintained—are now accustomed to imagine him as actually occupying a certain portion of space with a bodily organism, containing flesh, bones, and blood. The conception of physical facts and possibilities which modern science has established among us has unconsciously rendered any such imagination quite alien to us. Accordingly I believe that the weekly repetition of the Creed in most cases no longer suggests this idea either to the clergy or to the educated laity who repeat it. The meaning has changed for them gradually, without a shade of conscious unveracity at any state of the process. But that is because the words of the Creed present no definite barrier to the change: had the words of the Article been used, the case would have been quite different. As it is, a phrase, which was always in part a metaphor,★ has come to be understood as completely metaphorical or symbolical, by a perfectly smooth transition of thought.

A similar but slighter change has taken place in the common understanding of the phrase "descended into hell," which has lost the idea of

---

★ The apparent anthropomorphism of the phrase "at the right hand of God the Father" must have been intended figuratively by the framers of the Anglican formularies: as the first Article declares that God is "without body, parts, or passions."

downward movement—and even, perhaps, of spatial movement altogether—and come to mean simply "passed to the abode of departed spirits." The figure of local motion downward has been accepted without difficulty, from old habit and association—perhaps aided by some vague connexion between the known position of the buried bodies of the dead relatively to the living and the imagined position of their souls.★

I pass to another instance, where an important affirmation has undergone a distinct change of meaning, from the introduction of a qualification not originally intended.

A candidate for ordination as deacon is solemnly asked by the bishop, "Do you unfeignedly believe all the Canonical Scriptures of the Old and New Testament?" There seems to be no doubt that this was originally intended to import a belief in the truth of every statement in the Bible, the whole aggregate of books included in the Old and New Testament being regarded as literally the "Word of God." But as the development of historical method and scientific knowledge rendered it more and more difficult for educated persons to hold this belief, the phrase gradually came to be understood with a tacit limitation expressible by some such words, as "so far as they convey religious teaching." It is possible that this change originally involved some degree of deception,—the bishops and the common understanding of the Church taking the words in one sense, and a few exceptionally enlightened candidates taking them in the more limited sense, conscious that it would have been repudiated by the bishops and the Church generally. But it seems equally probable that the new meaning came in gradually without any such consciousness; and in any case it has now been recognized as admissible for more than a generation.

For when the matter came before the Ecclesiastical Courts in the trial of Dr. Rowland Williams for heresy (1862), the stricter view of the scope of the deacon's declaration seems to have been unhesitatingly rejected by

---

★ It is curious to note how the imagination—as distinct from the thought—of the region of departed spirits as being *beneath* the region of living men, still survives in the modern mind, notwithstanding the long domination of a conception of the physical universe that might have been expected to exclude it. We find it even in so intensely serious and profoundly modern a poem as Tennyson's *In Memoriam:*

> So, dearest, now thy brows are cold
> I see thee what thou art, and know
> Thy likeness to the wise below,
> Thy kindred with the great of old.

the judge of the Arches Court. Dr. Lushington held that the nature of the Old and New Testament "must be borne in mind in considering the extent of the obligation imposed by the words 'I do believe.'"* This expression, he said, "must be modified by the subject-matter,"—there must be a *bonâ fide* "belief that the Holy Scriptures contain everything necessary to salvation, and that to that extent they have the *direct* sanction of the Almighty." The view here expressed was illustrated and further defined in dealing with the particular charge that Dr. Williams' statements about the book of Daniel contradicted the declaration in the Deacon's Ordination Service. Dr. Williams had explicitly affirmed that the "admitted necessities of the case" undoubtedly bring our book of Daniel "as low as the reign of Epiphanes"; the writer of the book having "used a name traditionally sacred, with no deceptive intention, as a dramatic form which dignified his encouragement of his countrymen in their great struggle against Antiochus." All this, says the judge, "may be wholly erroneous, but . . . I do not see any repugnance to the deacon's declaration."†

I conceive that an Ecclesiastical Court may fairly be taken as an authorized interpreter of the meaning and scope of an ecclesiastical formula; so that any one who accepts the canonical books, in any real sense whatever, as a divinely-inspired source of religious teaching, may with perfect veracity make the deacon's declaration, although disbelieving many statements made in these books as to historical facts.

But in this appeal to judicial authority it is important to distinguish clearly between the *major* and the *minor* premiss of the judicial syllogism. I have more than once seen arguments to the following effect: "The legal obligations of a clergyman are a fair measure of his moral obligations; the essayists and reviewers were acquitted by the courts; therefore a clergyman may legally—and therefore morally—hold opinions similar to theirs, however apparently inconsistent with the Creeds he recites." And I understand Mr. Rashdall's reference to the failure of judicial prosecutions for heresy to imply reasoning of this kind; but it seems to me quite fallacious. In one sense, indeed, I think it plain that the legal obligation is the measure of the moral one; i.e., I think that a clergyman cannot be morally bound to take a stricter interpretation of his declarations and pledges than

---

* See *Ecclesiastical Judgments of the Privy Council,* by Brodrick and Fremantle, p. 256.
† *l.c.,* p. 259.

that adopted by the Ecclesiastical Courts in stating the general principles of their decisions. But it cannot reasonably be inferred that the writer of an essay is morally guiltless of holding—or even of designedly communicating—opinions that contravene his solemn affirmations, merely because this contravention cannot be proved from the language of the essay by the strict methods of proof required to justify a legal sentence. It is easy for a writer with any literary skill to suggest to his readers in a manner practically unmistakable, and persuasively commend to their acceptance, heretical opinions which he yet does not avow in the explicit and precise form required to bring them into demonstrable conflict with the Creeds and Articles; and there can be no doubt that the Essayists and Reviewers had repeatedly adopted this course.

I may give as an illustration Dr. Williams' language in regard to the particular doctrine with which I am primarily concerned in the present discussion. His article—which was a sympathetic review of Bunsen's *Biblical Researches*—contained the following sentences:* "Thus the incarnation becomes with our author as purely spiritual as it was with St. Paul. The Son of David by birth is the Son of God by the Spirit of holiness. What is flesh is born of flesh, and what is Spirit is born of Spirit." No intelligent reader can doubt that Dr. Williams designed to suggest that the accounts of the miraculous birth of Jesus are legendary, and that He was in reality the son of Joseph. Accordingly he was charged with contravening the statement in the Second Article that the Son of God "took man's nature in the womb of the Blessed Virgin." But his dexterous use of the language of St. Paul—who certainly shows no knowledge of the miraculous birth—had enabled him to suggest the desired conclusion without any explicit denial of the traditional doctrine; and the judge naturally finds it impossible to condemn what cannot be denied to be a "not unfair expression of the substance of what St. Paul wrote."† This non-condemnation, however, cannot reasonably be argued to imply that a clergyman is not bound to believe in the miraculous birth; since there can be no doubt that Dr. Williams would have been condemned at once if he had explicitly denied it.

To sum up: by a gradual introduction of a metaphorical or symbolic

---

* *Essays and Reviews*, p. 82.
† *Ecclesiastical Judgments*, p. 258.

meaning into words originally understood in a more literal sense, and by a gradual introduction of tacit qualifications and reserves into phrases originally understood in an absolute and unqualified sense, changes in some cases important have no doubt taken place in the common understanding of the Anglican formularies; and whether or not such changes have involved deception in the past—which I conjecture to be not the case for the most part—I hold that any person may now, without unveracity, use the phrases in the newer meaning. And I see no reason why similar changes should not take place in the future with perfect legitimacy. I quite admit that either process may conceivably be applied so as to involve substantial unveracity; but I do not think it possible to draw in general terms a clear line between the legitimate and the illegitimate introduction of new meanings in either way. The common understanding of language, changing with changes in knowledge and habitual sentiment, must be the test; but the appeal to this may in particular cases give a doubtful result. There are always likely to be differences of opinion on such questions among conscientious persons, which may be reduced, but can hardly be altogether removed, by frank and temperate discussion. Hence the decisions of Ecclesiastical Courts—taken with the limitation that I have explained—are useful as authoritatively declaring the limits of legitimate variation in the use of terms. But they are not the only means available for attaining this end. A general expression of opinion on the part of bishops or recognized theological experts—at any rate, if received with acquiescence by the Anglican clergy and laity generally—would have a similar effect. Such an expression of opinion has, in fact, taken place with regard to the damnatory clauses in the Athanasian Creed, declaring these to be applicable only to those who wilfully reject the doctrines of the Creed; and, however little any individual clergyman may think that this declaration represents the original meaning of the clauses, it would in my opinion be now over-scrupulous in him to make a difficulty about reciting the Creed on account of these clauses.

But, however difficult it may be in certain cases to decide exactly when a divergence in thought from the literal sense of any affirmation becomes illegitimate and evasive, it is easy to say that some divergences are quite beyond any defensible line; and that seems to me the case with the affirmation defended by Mr. Rashdall. The assertion that Jesus Christ was born of a virgin has a perfectly simple and definite negative meaning; it is based on well known and unmistakable statements by two evangelists, a belief in which it must certainly be understood to imply unless the opposite is expressly stated; it is impossible to conceive—and no one has ever suggested—any admissible qualification by which the phrase could be adapted to the thought of a man who believes that Jesus was the son of Joseph. Mr. Rashdall suggests that the phrase may be used to mean that Jesus was without sin from His birth; but I find it difficult to treat the suggestion seriously. A metaphor, to be undeceptive, must be accepted as such by hearers as well as speakers; whereas there is surely not the slightest chance that any part of any congregation would—without an express declaration that this was the speaker's meaning—understand the affirmation of the miraculous birth to mean an affirmation of the infant's sinlessness. And Mr. Rashdall hardly suggests that they would now so understand it; but he seems to think that they might be educated up to accept the meaning. I do not believe such education to be possible; but granting it possible, I submit that to save the statement from unveracity it must be made after the education has been performed, and not before.

It may be replied that if the Postnatalist makes his real opinion known, the mere repetition of the Creed becomes no longer unveracious, because there is no deception. I quite agree that if any one declares plainly the sense in which he utters any words, then, however alien this sense may be to the common understanding of the words, there is no substantial unveracity. But in order that his act may have this character the declaration must be made publicly; a private explanation to a bishop and an incumbent is not sufficient; it would only make them accomplices in deception. Further, I cannot consider that a false statement in the recital of a Creed is rendered unobjectionable by a public declaration of its falsity; because it is likely still to give a shock to the moral sentiment of a plain man, who cannot be expected to distinguish clearly between formal and substantial unveracity; moreover, the solemn utterance of untrue words will seem to him a mockery of sacred things and offend his religious sentiment. Still, if such an express public declaration were made, the responsibility for these consequences would be thrown, in a great measure, on the Church. The Postnatalists would have fairly and frankly challenged the Church to say whether it tolerated them or not; it would be for the Church to consider whether this toleration did not of necessity involve the removal of the Apostles' Creed from its place in the service.

In any case I admit fully that a Postnatalist clergyman, who has frankly stated his views to his congregation and to the world, is not open to the charge of unveracity in the sense in which I am here mainly concerned with it. But it is important to insist that for this purpose the declaration must be perfectly frank and explicit. A heretic cannot fairly argue that the common understanding of the Church has tolerated his heresy, because he—or someone holding similar views—has not been prosecuted, or has been prosecuted and acquitted, so long as the escape from legal penalties may be reasonably attributed to the absence of a candid and explicit statement of his opinions.*

Nor is it, I conceive, of any avail to urge that the belief in question has—at least for the Postnatalist, who is also a Trinitarian—"no spiritual importance." This is, indeed a consideration of much weight when the question is of his remaining in the Church and continuing to attend its services as a layman; but when it is a question of solemnly affirming a proposition without believing it, he ought to consider the significance of the belief to others rather than to himself. Now it cannot be denied that the rejection of the miraculous birth is, in the view of the great majority of Christians, a divergence of no light moment from "the faith delivered to the saints." And this prevalent opinion appears to me well founded. For if the methods of modern criticism are by any one allowed to prevail so far, against scriptural narratives and ecclesiastical tradition, as to lead to the rejection of the miraculous birth of Jesus, it must be an exceptionally constituted mind that can find the authority of the evangelists still sufficient to sustain the vast weight of Nicene Theology. Most of those who have gone so far will find themselves drawn further; other miraculous stories will have to be given up as legendary; the marvellous cures of Jesus will sink into remarkable cases of faith-healing, and the accounts of the post-resurrection apparitions into a remarkable ghost story, swollen into legend by the unconscious fictions of witnesses and reporters. Thus Christianity will soon come to have a purely ethical import, and the divine sonship of Jesus, so far as it is still affirmed, will only be affirmed in the sense of unique consciousness of the relation existing, essentially or ideally, between the human spirit and the divine. No doubt there is so

---

* As I have shown in the case of Dr. Williams, the failure of the prosecution of the Essayists and Reviewers in 1862 may be fairly attributed to this cause.

much friction on this inclined plane of thought that individuals may stop at almost any point: but of the general force of logic, impelling to the ultimate result that I have indicated, I can entertain no doubt.

Now I am far from any wish to disparage the form of religion resulting from the reduction of Christian dogma to this minimum; on the contrary, I should, in the present state of thought, welcome any increase of influence that it may obtain by fair advocacy; but I think that even Mr. Rashdall will agree with me in deprecating any attempt to pour this new wine into the old bottles of the Anglican formularies. And if so, it seems clearly unreasonable to ask the Church of England to throw over the Apostles' Creed, in order to admit to its ministry the handful of Postnatalists who stop at Postnatalism. But even assuming that this momentous breach with tradition is to lead to no further consequences, I should still urge—in the interest of religion, morality, and free thought at once—that it ought to be effected openly, and not through the stealthy and secret approaches recommended by Mr. Rashdall: that the new reformers should not profess loyalty to this time-honoured doctrine weekly with their lips, while their heart is far from it.

Mr. Rashdall dwells on the importance of maintaining and extending "the Christian κοινωνία," and on the "spiritual and social loss of multiplied schism." I may remind the reader that the argument of the preceding address does not lead to external separation as a necessary result of intellectual disagreement; quite the contrary. At the same time, I think that Mr. Rashdall's language misrepresents the actual conditions of thought and social life; his ideas of "unity" and "schism" are either too far behind the age or too far in advance of it—or perhaps both at once. External unity is a hollow form without spiritual unity, unity of thought and feeling; and spiritual unity will only be completely possible for the modern mind when competent students of theology have come to an agreement on fundamental questions of principle and method, similar to that which has been already attained by students of physical science. Suppose this result reached, then the question of substituting a single for a multiple ecclesiastical organization becomes a mere question of mechanism—I do not say unimportant, but certainly of secondary importance from a religious point of view. On the other hand, unitl this result is reached unity cannot but remain a sentiment, an aspiration, an unrealized ideal; though doubtless the sentiment may be developed, and the realization of the ideal brought nearer, by moral as well as intellectual methods;—by the cultivation of sympathy between different churches, by the cordial co-operation of their members in philanthropic work, by temperateness in controversy, by a sustained desire to recognize the merits and do justice to the motives of opponents. Progress is already being made in this direction, and the spiritual and social evils of schism are being thereby steadily diminished; but this progress, I conceive, will be aided, rather than impeded, by such external separation as will allow teaching to be candid, forms of prayer to be adapted to the real beliefs of the worshippers, and clerical pledges to be taken and fulfilled in the sense in which they are commonly understood. I quite agree with Mr. Rashdall that under no conditions would it be desirable that a clergyman should flaunt before a comparatively uneducated audience novel opinions that would shock and perplex them; but he should be in a position to speak frankly to thoughtful members of his flock, and such frank speaking should be reconcilable with the solemn expression of beliefs which his office prescribes. The Preacher has said that there is "a time to speak and a time to keep silence," and this ancient wisdom is not yet antiquated. But he has not said that there is a time to speak truly and a time to speak falsely; and I think that, in religious matters, the common sense of Christendom will reject this addition to the familiar proverb.

VII

LUXURY

I HAVE chosen Luxury for the subject of my address this evening; because I think that the employment of wealth, in what we should agree to call luxurious expenditure, is a source of considerable perplexity to moral persons who find themselves in the possession of an income obviously more than sufficient for the needs of their physical existence, and for the provision of the instruments necessary to their work in life. Such persons commonly wish to do what common morality regards as right; yet for the most part they cannot deny that they live in luxury; while at the same time it can hardly be denied that luxurious living is commonly thought to be in some degree censurable. We should be surprised to hear an earnest and thoughtful man say, except jocosely, that it was part of his plan of life to live in luxury; or to hear an earnest and thoughtful father, toiling to accumulate by industry adequate wealth for his children, say that he wished to enable them to live in luxury. Yet often there would be no

An address delivered to the University Hall Guild, London, January, 1894; and subsequently to the Cambridge Ethical Society.

doubt that the habits of his life, and the habits and expectations which he is allowing his children to form, are habits and expectations of luxurious living.

Possibly some of my hearers may think that this is only the familiar phenomenon of human frailty; that the most moral persons are continually doing many things which they know to be wrong, and that luxurious living is only one of these many things. But I submit that it would be difficult to find a parallel case in the familiar errors and shortcomings of moral persons. For these errors and shortcomings are mostly occasional deflections from the way in which they regularly walk, due to transient victories of impulse over settled purpose. Doubtless appetite, resentment, vanity, egoism, frequently lead the most earnest persons astray; but it is commonly only for a brief interval, after which they reject and repudiate the seductive impulse and return to the path of reason and duty. But the luxurious living of the high-minded and earnest among the possessors of wealth is obviously not an occasional deflection of this kind: it is a high-road on which they travel day after day and year after year, systematically and—I was going to say comfortably, but that would not be quite true; my point rather is that they travel it with a certain amount—I think at the present time a growing amount—of moral uneasiness and perplexity.

Here, perhaps, some one may think that this perplexity, if it is a perplexity, is one which interests only a very limited circle, at least from a moral point of view. It may be said that the difficulty that the rich find in trying to enter the kingdom of heaven was long ago made known to us by the highest authority; but that, fortunately for the human race, this particular obstacle affects only a few, for whose moral troubles we can hardly be called on to feel much sympathy, since to get rid of the obstacle is only too easy. I think, however, that this would be a hasty and superficial judgment. No doubt it is only a small minority of persons who are privileged to dwell in marble halls, adorned with damask hangings, and surrounded by acres of park and garden-beds; who are liable to dinners costing two guineas a head, and who habitually wear whatever substitute for purple the æsthetic fashion of this modern age prescribes. But if luxurious living is morally censurable, the censure must extend far beyond the limits of the few thousand persons who enjoy these privileges; it must extend to all who watch this glorious profusion with mingled sympathy and envy, struggle and long to get a share of it whenever opportunity offers, and meanwhile pay it the homage of cheap imitation. Indeed, if the sin of luxurious living, like many other sins, lies mainly in the spirit and intention of expenditure, it would be easy to write an apologue that should be the reverse of the tale of the widow's mite, and show how the spirit of luxury may be fully manifested in the expenditure of sixpence on lollipops or feathers or gin.

But further, even if it were granted that the costly luxuries of the rich are really the only kind of luxuries that can possibly deserve the unfavourable judgment of the moralist, it would still be important to all classes of the community that this censure should be well considered and discriminating. For any material change in the expenditure in question would inevitably, in one way or another, have economic and social effects of a far-reaching kind, however it was brought about; and if such a change ever should be brought about, it will be largely due to the pressure of the moral opinions and sentiments of persons other than the rich.

My aim, then, this evening will be to arrive at as clear a view as possible on the following questions: (1) What luxury is; (2) Why and how far it is deserving of censure.

Let us begin by considering the definition of the term. Political economists sometimes use the term "luxury" in a wide sense, to include all forms of private consumption of wealth not necessary for the health or working efficiency of the consumer; all consumption—to put it otherwise—which is neither directly nor indirectly productive, and which, therefore, would be uneconomical, if we regarded a man merely as an industrial machine. It may seem, however, that we should keep nearer to ordinary thought and language by recognizing one or more kinds of expenditure intermediate between luxuries on the one hand and necessaries on the other. Certainly we commonly speak of "luxuries, comforts and necessaries"; or, again, of "luxuries, decencies, and necessaries of life"; and I think we may get a clearer idea of what we mean by "luxury" if we examine its relation to each of these intermediate terms.

When we reflect on the ordinary distinction between "luxuries" and "comforts," the difference seems to be this: "comforts" are means of protection against slight pains and annoyances such as do not materially injure health or interfere with efficiency—such annoyances as we call "discomforts";—"luxuries," on the other hand, are sources of positive pleasure whose absence would not cause discomfort. It is commonly, I think, not difficult for an individual to apply this distinction in his own case, so far as his feelings at any particular time are concerned. Thus, when I take a long railway journey on a frosty day, a thick great-coat is necessary to me, because without it I am likely to catch a cold which will impair my efficiency; a railway rug is a comfort, because without it I shall be disagreeably cold from the knees downward; a fur cloak is a luxury. But reflection shows that the difference on which this distinction turns is very largely an affair of habit, since the privation of luxuries that have become habitual usually causes discomfort and annoyance. We are told that a famous Roman epicure—Apicius—committed suicide when he had reduced his fortune to eighty thousand pounds, feeling that life was not worth living on this meagre scale; and though this is an extreme case, it is generally recognized that a rapid fall from great to moderate wealth is liable to cause positive discomfort from the sudden break of luxurious habits that it entails. But is is not, perhaps, generally recognized how very far-reaching this effect of habit is, and how largely what we call comforts are—apart from habit—really luxuries. I suppose there can be no doubt that the vast majority of Englishmen might without discomfort dispense through life with all such nervous stimulants as tea, coffee, alcohol, and tobacco—at any rate, if they had been reared from infancy without them. I do not say this without experience. I lived myself in perfect comfort between the ages of twelve and nineteen, drinking only water at all meals; and I remember that I could not imagine why people took the trouble to manufacture tea, coffee, and wine. Yet the most hard-headed modern economist would not deprive an old woman of her tea in the workhouse; and I am told that whatever deterrent effect the prospect of imprisonment under present conditions has on our criminal classes depends largely on the deprivation of their habitual alcohol and tobacco.

It seems clear, then, that the line between luxuries and comforts is necessarily a shifting one. The commonest comforts might—apart from the effect of habit—be classed as luxuries; the most expensive luxuries may, through habit, become mere comforts, in the sense that they cannot be dispensed with without annoyance.

We have now to observe that often the annoyance which the loss of wealth causes to the loser arises solely from the fall in social position and reputation which it is rightly or wrongly believed to entail. This leads me to my second distinction:—that between "luxuries" and the "decencies" of life. I here use "decencies" in a wide sense, to mean all commodities beyond necessaries which we consume to avoid not physical discomfort, but social disrepute. Perhaps I may make my distinction between "decencies" and "comforts" clear by a homely illustration. Many men, I believe, find that their coats, hats, and boots are liable to be condemned by domestic criticism as not "decent" to wear in public, just when they have become most thoroughly adapted to the peculiarities of the wearer's organism, and so most thoroughly comfortable. Half a century ago I believe that boots were altogether a "decency" rather than a comfort for a valuable and thriving part of the population of our island; at least a political economist* of that date tells us that a "Scotch peasant wears shoes to preserve not his feet, but his station in society."

It will, therefore, be clear at once that just as the line between "luxuries" and "comforts" varies almost indefinitely with the habits of individuals, the distinctions between "luxuries" and "decencies" varies similarly with the customs and opinions of classes.

Now, if we are passing judgment on an individual accused of luxury in a bad sense, or giving advice to one desirous of avoiding it, the consideration of his formed habits and the customs of his class must be taken into account. It may sometimes be even unwise in him to break habits which it would yet have been wise not to have formed; for a struggle with habit sometimes involves a material temporary decrease of efficiency, and a hard-working man reasonably objects to impair his efficiency. The principle is no doubt a dangerous one, and easily abused; but I do not think we can deny its legitimacy within strict limits. So, again, though we should usually admire an individual who breaks through a custom of useless expenditure we should usually shrink from imposing this as an absolute duty, and sometimes should even condemn it as unwise. A fight with custom is, like other fights, inspiriting and highly favourable to the development of moral courage; but usually, like other fights, it cannot be carried on without cost and sacrifice of some kind; and it is the part of a wise man to count the cost before undertaking it, and to measure his resources against the strength of the adversary.

But at present I only mention these considerations to exclude them. I do not now wish to consider how we are to judge individuals, but rather

* Senior.

how we are to judge habits and customs regarded as social facts. For such habits and customs are being modified continually though slowly; and if they are bad, it is desirable that the pressure of public opinion should in one way or another be brought to bear to modify them. "They may say it is the Persian fashion, but let it be changed," as Shakespeare has it.

From this point of view I think it convenient to avoid the necessarily shifting and relative definitions of decencies and comforts, and to fall back on the simpler distinction between "luxuries" and "necessaries"; extending, however, the term necessaries to include expenditure required by such habits and customs as we consider generally necessary to physical or moral well-being; e.g., habits of due cleanliness and such customs in respect of decency—in a strict sense—as we judge important, if not indispensable, to morality. This extension is, I think, required by ordinary usage, for no one would apply the term "luxurious" in an unfavourable meaning to expenditure of this kind. And I think we shall further agree that the term is not properly applicable to expenditure that increases a man's efficiency in the performance of his industrial or social function, so long as the increase of efficiency is not obtained at a disproportionate cost. But this requirement of due proportion between expenditure and increase of efficiency should be kept carefully in view, because in all kinds of work it is possible to increase efficiency really but wastefully by adding instruments which are of *some* use, but are not worth their cost. In the application of wealth, by which a competent man of business *makes* hs income, this proportion of efficiency to cost is easily estimated, and clearly unremunerative conveniences—e.g., machines that clearly cost more labour than they save—are carefully excluded; but in the application of wealth by which an income is *spent,* this economic care is often thrown aside, and instruments are purchased which, while not absolutely useless for the purchaser's ends, are at any rate of very little use in proportion to their cost,—not unfrequently of so little use that they do not even compensate the loss of time and trouble spent in taking care of them. May I take an illustration from my own calling? I have heard of a scholar who did good work in his youth and attained fame and promotion; but then his work slackened and stopped. On inquiry this was found to be due not to laziness, but to his increasing absorption in the task of buying, housing, binding, classifying, arranging, and looking after the splendid collection of books that he had formed to aid his researches.

For this form of luxury, these inconvenient conveniences, there is no defence. But I dwell on it now because, ever since moral reflection began in Europe, there have been thoughtful persons who have held that the customary luxurious expenditure of the rich on food, clothes, houses, furniture, carriages, horses, etc., consisted mainly in conveniences that were really quite uneconomic, because one way or another they caused more trouble and annoyance than they saved to their possessor. I will quote an expression of this view from a source which may surprise some of my hearers; i.e., from a work* by the founder of the long line of modern political economists who are commonly supposed to exalt wealth too exclusively, and to value it unduly. Adam Smith, in 1759, wrote that "wealth and greatness are mere trinkets of frivolous utility, no more adapted for procuring ease of body or tranquility of mind than the tweezer-cases of the lover of toys; and, like them, too, more troublesome to the person who carries them about with him than all the advantages they can afford him are commodious. . . . In ease of body and peace of mind all the different ranks of life are nearly upon a level, and the beggar who suns himself by the side of the highway possesses that security which kings are fighting for."

I have quoted this not because I believe it to be really true, but because it is interesting to find that Adam Smith believed it, and because it was a tolerably prevalent belief in his age. There is a story told by a writer of this period which may serve as another illustration: a story of a Persian king, afflicted with a strange malady, who had been informed by a wise physician that he could be cured by wearing the shirt of a perfectly happy man. It was at first supposed that there could be no difficulty in finding such a man among the upper ten thousand of Persia; but the court was searched in vain, and the city was searched in vain; and the messengers sent to prosecute the search through the country found that landowners and farmers had all their sorrows and anxieties. At length the searchers met a labourer, singing as he came home from work. Struck with his gaiety, they questioned him as to his happiness. He professed himself perfectly happy. They probed him with minute inquiries, but no flaw in his happiness was revealed. The long-sought remedy seemed to be in their hands; but, alas! the happy man wore *no* shirt.

* *Theory of Moral Sentiments,* part iv., chap. i.

Well, I think this story will show how far the thought of the nineteenth century has travelled from the view of life that was prevalent in the age of Adam Smith and Rousseau. Perhaps it has travelled a little too far. Adam Smith was—what Rousseau certainly was not—a shrewd, calm, and disengaged observer of the facts of civilized life. He sometimes, as here, gives the rein to rhetoric, but he never lets it carry him away. And I think that his view contains an important element of truth; that it signalizes a real danger of wasted effort, growing in importance as the arts of industry grow, against which civilized man has to guard. I think that every thoughtful person, in planning his expenditure, ought to keep this danger in view, and avoid the multiplication of useless, or nearly useless, instruments— houses larger than he at all needs, servants whose services are not materially time-saving, a private carriage when walking is ordinarily better for his health and adequate for his business, and many minor superfluities which absorb the margin of income that would otherwise be available for results of real utility. Still, taking Adam Smith's statement in its full breadth, I cannot but regard it as a paradox containing more error than truth. I see no reason to doubt that the steady aim of civilized man to increase the pleasures of life by refining and complicating their means and sources— an aim which in all ages has stimulated and directed the development of industry and commerce—has been to a great extent a successful aim, so far as its immediate end is concerned.

Let us, then, putting out of sight expenditure prompted by bad habits, or imposed by useless customs, and expenditure on illusory conveniences that give more trouble than they save, concentrate our attention on luxury successful in its immediate aims—i.e., consumption that increases pleasure without materially promoting health or efficiency; and let us consider how far and on what grounds this may reasonably be thought deserving of censure. Now—if we put aside the paradoxes of stoical moralists who deny that pleasure is a good—the arguments against increasing an individual's pleasure by superfluous consumption seem to be chiefly three. It may be urged, first, that the process usually injures his health in the long run; secondly, that it impairs his efficiency for the performance of his social functions; thirdly, that the labour he causes to be spent in providing him with the means of pleasure would have produced more happiness, on the whole, if it had been spent in providing the means of pleasure for others. The first two of these considerations form the main staple of the older arguments against luxury; the third is more prominent in modern thought. I will briefly consider each in turn.

On the first of these heads—the effect of luxury on health—there is much need to meditate, but little for a layman to say. That persons of wealth and leisure are in danger of excess in sensual indulgences; that this excess is continually being committed; that it is not difficult to avoid it by care and self-control; that those who do not avoid it are palpably foolish; what more is there to say for one who is not a physician?

I remember that in one of the most polished and pointed poems that Pope ever wrote, he speaks of his father as having had a long life—"Healthy by temperance and by exercise." The line, you see, is neither polished nor pointed; and I used to wonder how Pope's fine taste ever came to admit such a platitude, until I read the brilliant chapter in Trevelyan's *Early History of Charles James Fox,* on the manners of London society in the middle of the eighteenth century. It then occurred to me that the fact of a man of means having lived to old age, "healthy by temperance and by exercise," may have seemed to Pope so rare and remarkable that its bare statement would be impressive without any verbal adornments. Well, I hope that this has been changed in the nineteenth century; but I leave the question to the social historian; the philosopher may be permitted to pass on, only remarking that the folly of sacrificing health to sensual indulgence is not the distinctive privilege of any social class. I remember that Pope, whom I have just quoted, sneers at legislation that spares the vices of the rich, "and hurls the thunders of the laws on gin." But the legislators might have answered, that while champagne and burgundy were slaying their thousands, "gin" was slaying its tens of thousands.

But, secondly, it is urged that, whithout positively injuring health, the refinement and complication of the means of physical enjoyment tend to diminish efficiency for work. Looking closer at this argument, we find that it combines two distinct objections: one is that luxury makes men *lazy,* disinclined for labour; the other is that it makes them *soft,* incapable of the prolonged, strenuous exertion and the patient endurance of disagreeable incidents which most kinds of effective work require. On the point of laziness I will speak presently. As regards softness, the objection has this element of truth in it—that the powers of sustained exertion and endurance are developed, like other powers, by practice, and that the lives of the poor provide normally an unsought training of these powers from childhood upwards, which has to be supplied artificially, if at all, in the lives of the rich. But I think experience shows that the objection is not very serious, at least for our race. Certainly, Englishmen brought up in luxury seem usually to show an adequate capacity of exertion and endurance when any strong motive is supplied for the exercise of these qualities.

We come, then, to the question of laziness, meaning by laziness a disposition to work clearly less than is good for one's self and others. There can be no doubt that the luxurious tend as a class to be lazy; the possession of the means of sensual enjoyment without labour disposes average men, if not to absolute inertia, at any rate to short working hours and long holidays. On the other hand, if luxury makes men lazy, the prospect of luxury makes them work; and if we balance the two effects on motive, I think there can be no doubt that, other things remaining the same, a society from which luxury was effectually excluded would be lazier than a society that admitted it. If it be said that the desire of luxury is a low motive, I might answer in the manner in which one of the wisest of English moralists—Butler—speaks of resentment. I should say that "it were much to be wished that men would act on a better principle"; but that if you could suppress the desire of luxury without altering human nature in other respects, you would probably do harm, because you would diminish the general happiness by increasing laziness.

This argument is, I think, decisive from a political point of view, as a defence of a social order that allows great inequalities in the distribution of wealth for consumption. But when I hear it urged as conclusive from an ethical point of view, I am reminded of Lord Melbourne's answer to a friend whom he consulted, when premier, as to the bestowal of a vacant garter. His friend said, "Why not take it yourself? No one has a better claim." "Well, but," said Lord Melbourne, "I don't see what I am to gain by bribing myself." The answer is cynical in expression, but it contains a lesson for some who profess a higher moral standard than Lord Melbourne was in the habit of professing. For when we have decided that the toleration of luxury as a social fact is indispensable to the full development of human energy, the ethical question still remains for each individual, whether it is indispensable for him; whether, in order to get himself to do his duty, he requires to bribe himself by a larger share of consumable wealth than falls to the common lot. And if one answers the question in the affirmative, one must admit one's self to belong to the class of persons characterized by George Eliot as "people whose high ideals are not required to account for their actions."

Further, the moral censor of luxury may rejoin that he admits the danger of repressing luxury without repressing laziness, and is quite willing to divide his censure equally between the two. He may even grant that, of the two, more stress should be laid on the discouragement of idleness; and that the moral repression of luxury can only be safely attempted by slow degrees, so far as we succeed in substituting nobler motives for activity—i.e., so far as we can make it natural and customary for all men, whatever their means, to choose some social function and devote themselves strenuously to its excellent performance.

But if the censor takes this line—and I think it practically a wise line—he by implication admits the inconclusiveness of the argument against luxury as an inducement to idleness; for it implies that the two are separable, and that idleness, like softness and disease, is not an inevitable concomitant of luxurious living, but only a danger that may be guarded against.

I come, then, to the third argument—viz., that a man who lives luxuriously consumes what would have produced more happiness if he had left it to be consumed by others. It is to be observed that this is an argument not against luxury itself, so far as it is successful luxury, but against its unequal distribution; it is an argument in favour of cheap luxuries for the many instead of costly luxuries for the few. And this, I think, is generally the case with the modern censures of luxurious living as contrasted with the more ancient censures; the modern attack is rather directed against inequality in the distribution of the means of enjoyment than against the general principle of heightening the pleasures of life by refining and elaborating their means and sources; or, at any rate, if this elaboration is attacked, it is only because it involves, from a social point of view, a waste of labour. But though this makes a fundamental difference in the *grounds* of the attack, it does not make much difference in its *objects;* since it is the consumer of costly luxuries who in all ages has stood in the forefront of the controversy and borne the brunt of moral censure. Accordingly, in the little I have yet to say of luxury, I shall use the term in the special sense of costly luxury.

It must be admitted that this third objection, so far as it is valid at all, is more inevitable than the preceding ones. A man may avoid disease by care and self-control; he may avoid idleness and softness by bracing exercise of his faculties, physical and mental, while still systematically heightening his enjoyment of existence by elaborate and complex means of pleasure; but just as he cannot both eat his cake and have it, so he cannot both eat his cake and arrange that other men should eat it too, or that they should consume the simpler products of the baker's art which might have resulted from the same labour.

Need I say a word about the hoary fallacy that a man by eating his cake provides employment—and therefore cake, or at least bread—for the baker? "Time was," as Shakespeare says, "that when the brains were out the man would die"; and as the brains have been out of this fallacy generations ago, I shall consider it as slain, even though it still walks the earth with inextinguishable vitality, and occasionally reappears in the writings of the most superior persons. I shall venture to assume that, speaking generally, a man benefits others by rendering services to them, and not by requiring them to render services to him.

Can we accept it as a generally satisfactory defence of the costly luxuries of the few that, owing to the exquisite delicacy of the palates of certain individuals, the general happiness is best promoted by the consumption of cake being reserved to them? that they are to be regarded, in fact, as the organ of humanity for the appreciation of cake? There is some truth in this, if we are considering a *sudden* change; since experience shows that refined luxury is liable to be wasted on persons suddenly transplanted into it late in life. But the arguments do not go far, since the same experience shows that the task of educating any class up to the standard of capacity for enjoying luxury, which is reached on the average by the wealthiest class of the age, is not a difficult task, though it requires time. It is, indeed, in most cases, an educational problem peculiarly easy of solution. Hence I do not think this consideration can weigh much against the broad fact that, even in the case of successful luxury, increase in the means of enjoyment consumed by the same individual is accompanied by increase of enjoyment in a continually diminishing ratio; so that inequality in the distribution of consumption is uneconomic from a social point of view.

A really valid defence of luxury, then, must be found, if at all, in some service which the luxurious consumer as such renders to the non-luxurious. That is, it must be shown that so-called luxury is not really such, according to our definition, but is a provision necessary for the efficient performance of some social function.

From this point of view it is sometimes said that luxury is a kind of social insurance against disaster, as providing a store of commodity on which society can draw when widespread economic losses occur through war or industrial disturbance. Such disasters would no doubt cause far graver distress if they fell on a body of human beings who had among them hardly more than the necessaries of life; but though this is an argument for habitually producing a certain amount of commodities not required for health or efficiency, it is not a strong argument for distributing them unequally. The social surplus required might be nearly as well created by the cheap superfluities of the many as by the costly superfluities of the few.

Passing over other inadequate defences of luxury, I come to the only one to which I am disposed to attach weight—viz., that inequality in the distribution of superfluous commodities is required for the social function of advancing culture, enlarging the ideal of human life, and carrying it towards ever fuller perfection. Here it seems desirable to draw a distinction between the two main elements of culture—(1) the apprehension and advancement of knowledge, and (2) the appreciation and production of beauty, as it is in respect of the latter that defence is most obviously needed. No doubt in the past learning and science have been largely advanced by men of wealth; no doubt, also, the scholar or researcher at the present day requires continually more elaborate provision in the way of libraries, museums, apparatus. But these we shall properly regard not as luxuries but as the instruments of a profession or calling of high social value; and, generally speaking, there seems no reason why the pursuit of knowledge should suffer if the expenditure of the student, inclusive of the funds devoted to the instruments of his calling, were kept free from all costly luxury and "high thinking" universally accompanied by "plain living." And the same view may be, to a great extent at least, legitimately taken of the expenditure on the pursuit of knowledge incurred by that large majority of educated persons who can hardly hope to contribute materially to the scientific progress of mankind: so far as this expenditure tends directly or indirectly to increase the efficiency of their intellectual activities. Some portion of this may no doubt be wasted in the gratification of idle curiosity, so as to leave no intellectual profit behind;

and theoretically we must except this portion from our defence of costly expenditure on intellectual pursuits. But I do not think that this exception is practically very important, considering the hesitation that a wise man will always feel in pronouncing on the uselessness of any knowledge.

Can we similarly defend the costly expenditure of the rich on the cultivation and satisfaction of æsthetic sensibilities—on literature regarded as a fine art, on music and the drama, on paintings and sculptures, on ornamental buildings and furniture, on flowers and trees and landscape gardening of all kinds? Such expenditure is actually much larger in amount than that incurred in the pursuit of knowledge: and in considering it we reach, I think, the heart of this ancient controversy on luxury. Here, however, I have to confess that personal insight and experience fail me. I only worship occasionally in the outer court of the temple of beauty, and so I do not feel competent to hold the brief for luxury on the ground of its being a necessary condition of æsthetic progress. But though I cannot hold the brief I am prepared, as a member of the jury of educated persons, to give a verdict in favour of the defendant; so far, at least, as a sincere love of beauty is the predominant motive of the costly expenditure defended. I find that the study of history leads me continually to contemplate with sympathy and satisfaction the opulence and luxury of the few amid the hard lives of the many, because it presents itself as the practically necessary soil in which beauty and the love of beauty grow and develop; and because I see how, when new sources of high and refined delight have thus been produced, the best and most essential of their benefits extend by degrees from the few to the many, and become abiding possessions of the race. It is possible that in the future we may carry on artistic and æsthetic development successfully on the basis of public and collective effort, and dispense with the lavish and costly private expenditure of the few; but till we are convinced that this is likely—and I am not yet convinced—I think we should not hamper the progress of this priceless element of human life by any censure or discouragement of luxurious living, so long as it aims at the ends and keeps within the limits which I have endeavoured briefly to determine.

VIII

THE PURSUIT OF CULTURE

WHEN I was invited to deliver an incidental lecture to the students of the London School of Ethics and Social Philosophy, it seemed to me desirable to choose a subject that on the one hand should have an interest for students of Ethics, from a practical as well as theoretical point of view; and on the other hand, should not be customarily included—or, at least, only introduced in a very cursory and subordinate way—in the systematic treatment of Ethics. It seemed to me that the pursuit of culture as an ideal would fulfil these two conditions. Culture is a fundamentally important part of the human good that practical morality aims at promoting; at the same time, its importance in the general view of practical morality and philanthropy has grown very much during the last generation, with the enlargement of our conception of the prospective greatness of human life to be lived on this earth. I think no more remarkable change has ever taken place in human thought than this enlargement, due to the

An address delivered before the London School of Ethics and Social Philosophy on October 24th, 1897.

advance of science, especially of the historical sciences—geology, evolutional biology, archaeology, and anthropology, and the comprehensive but still rudimentary science sociology, which has taken nearly a century to get itself fairly born. The mundane life of the individual is as transient as ever; but the mundane life of the larger whole of which he is a part—the life of the human race—now spreads out before our imagination as all but infinte in its probable duration and its possibilities of development. Its past life is reckoned by tens of thousands of years: and the gloomiest forecasts of physicists as to the cooling of the sun allow it more millions of future years than I need try to count. Thus the problem of making human life on earth a better thing has become more and more clearly the dominant problem for morality, comprehending almost all minor problems, and determining the lines on which their solution is to be sought; and in the doubtless imperfect conception we form of this betterment, mental culture, which,—according to usage, I shall speak of briefly as culture,—has, as I said, a prominent place.

And the dominance of this problem has been further established by the change in current political ideas, of which our newspapers have long been so full,—the reaction against the individualism of the earlier political economists, which left the culture of the individual to his self-interest well understood, or, in the case of children, to parental affection, and merely aimed at protecting individuals and parents against interference in its pursuit. The enlarged conception of social and political duty which is now prevalent is impelling us with increasing force to promote positively the attainment of a good life for all;—through the action of the State, so far as experience shows this to be prudent, but also through private and voluntarily associated effort, outside and apart from, or in co-operation with, government. And this good life, as I have said, means for us a cultivated life, a life in which culture is in some degree attained and exercised.

Indeed, I think it may be said that the promotion of culture, in one form or another, is more and more coming to be recognized as the main moral justification for the luxurious expenditure of the rich. Observe that in saying this I wish clearly to distinguish the *moral* from the *political* justification. I have no hankering after sumptuary laws; and men being what they are, I have no doubt that the liberty to spend one's income luxuriously is—quite apart from any question of culture—an indispensable spring of economic progress. But what men ought to do is often very different from what they ought to be made to do. And if culture, like the greater goods, Religion and Morality, could be equally well promoted by scanty and restricted personal expenditure, it would seem to me—in view of the multiple evils of the penury around us—a clear moral duty for most persons with ample means to restrict their expenditure to the minimum necessary for the health, and the efficiency in professional or social work, of themselves and their families. The superfluity could then be spent in any of the ways of relieving distress which the Charity Organization Society would sanction; and in spite of the severity commonly attributed to that society, such sanctioned ways of spending are, I can assure you, both numerous and absorbent of funds. What stands in the way of this moral judgment is the widespread conviction that the lavish expenditure of the rich on the elements of culture, the means of developing and gratifying the love of knowledge and the love of beauty in all their various forms, meets an important social need,—wastefully no doubt, but still more effectively than it could at present be met in any other way; since the gain in knowledge and in elevated and refined delight obtained through this expenditure does not remain with the rich alone, but extends in a number of ways to other classes. Whether this conviction is sound or not I do not now consider: I only refer to it as illustrating the importance that we have come to attach to the notion of culture in our moral judgments.

And this comes out more clearly if we note what among the advantages which the rich actually derive from their superfluous expenditure— I mean expenditure not needed for health or efficiency—the genuine philanthropists among them are keenly desirous to give to others less fortunate. Surely—apart from the general and technical education required for economic efficiency—they consist almost entirely in the means of developing the elevated faculties and refined sensibilities which we include in the notion of culture. I do not mean that such a philanthropist would object to manual labourers feasting on grouse and champagne—as certain miners in the North were once said to do when wages were high—but he would not make efforts and sacrifices to spread these delicacies. Perhaps you may say that if wealthy philanthropists really put so high a value on culture, they would not spend so much of their wealth in giving themselves pleasant things which have little or nothing to do with culture. I might answer this in various ways. I might dwell on the tyranny of custom, and the conventional forms in which the time-honoured virtue of hospitality necessarily has to express itself. But perhaps the answer that goes deepest is that suggested by an old remark that the precept "Love thy neighbour as thyself" might—when it has attained general acceptance and serious efforts are made to fulfil it—be advantageously supplemented by the converse precept "Love thyself as thy neighbour": since a genuine regard for our neighbour—when not hampered by the tyranny of custom— prompts us to give him what we think really good for him; whereas natural self-regard prompts us to give ourselves what we like. Thus the spontaneous expression of altruism, rather than the spontaneous expression of egoism, corresponds to our deepest judgment, the judgment of our best self, as to the good and evil in human life.

If it were needful to give further more detailed proof of this growing recognition of the importance of culture, and the growing desire for its wider diffusion, I might draw attention to several different features in recent social movements. I might point, e.g., to the burning question of the "eight hours day," and the eagerness shown by the advocates of the workmen's side in this controversy to convince the public that it is really leisure they want for their clients, and not merely additional wages. No impartial outsider objects to their getting as much wages as the conditions of industry may allow; but they know that the demand for leisure to lead a more cultivated life will stir the keenest sympathy of lookers on. I might remind you of the resolution recently passed at a Socialistic Congress, that University education should be effectively open to all classes of the community, from the highest to the lowest; for even an extravagance of this kind is a straw that shows how strongly the current of opinion is flowing. I might refer to the efforts to render picture-galleries and museums of art really available for the delight and instruction of the poorer classes of the community; and I might point to what is sometimes attacked as the "encroachment of primary education on the province of secondary education"; which is, at any rate, evidence of the widespread determination to aim, even in elementary teaching, at something more than the *minimum* required for economic efficiency.

I only suggest these topics, as they are familiar to us all from the daily papers. I have said enough to show the growing importance of culture in our common conception of human good, in the ideal that morality aims at realizing. What I propose in the remainder of the present discourse is not to discuss the methods by which culture is to be promoted and diffused, but to free this fundamental notion, so far as possible, from obscurity and ambiguity, so that our philanthropic efforts to promote culture may have a clear and precise aim.

The question, what is culture? carries the thought of a man of my age irresistibly back to the delightful writer, who made the term familiar as a household word to the English reading public a generation ago—Matthew Arnold. I know that his poems are not forgotten by a younger generation, and I hope his essays are not forgotten either;—at any rate the less controversial of them, since the interest of controversy is usualy somewhat ephemeral. I know no writings in English that plead the cause of literary culture with an earnestness so light and graceful, and so persuasive a charm. It was early in the sixties that he began his efforts to penetrate the hide of self-complacency which, then as now, was a characteristic feature of his fellow-countrymen; and to make us feel the want of true culture in all the three classes into which he divided our society—Barbarians, Philistines, and Populace. He told us—he was never tired of telling us, and his style could make the most incessant iteration tolerable if not agreeable—he set forth to us in memorable phrases what culture was, and what great benefits we should gain if we would only turn and seek it with our whole heart. Unfortunately, Matthew Arnold was not—as he humorously confessed—a systematic thinker with philosophical principles duly coherent and interdependent; and consequently it is not surprising that he did not always mean the same thing by culture; indeed it is interesting to watch his conception expanding and contracting elastically, as he passes from phase to phase of a long controversy.

When his preaching began he appeared to mean by culture merely a knowledge of and taste for fine literature, and the refinement of feeling and manners which he considered to spring naturally from this source. Thus, when he remarks regretfully that the English aristocracy has declined somewhat from the "admirable" and "consummate" culture which it had attained in the eighteenth century, what he regrets is the time when the oracle of polite society—Lord Chesterfield—could tell the son whom he was training for a political career, that "Greek and Roman learning is the most necessary ornament which it is shameful not to be master of," and bid the nascent diplomatist "let Greek without fail share some part of every day." And Arnold here seems to signify by culture almost entirely the æsthetic value and effect of the study of fine literature and not its value for thought: since he speaks of a "high reason" and a "fine culture" as two distinct things, and tells the middle class—his "Philistines"—that they want both "culture" which aristocracy has, and "ideas" which aristocracy has not. But as the controversy went on and waxed a little hot, the limits of the notion came to be greatly enlarged. When John Bright sneered at culture as a "smattering of two dead languages," and when Mr. Frederick Harrison, in his "stringent manner," said that culture was a desirable quality in a critic of new books, but a poor thing when you came to active politics, Arnold was moved to unfold a much wider and deeper view of the essential quality of this divine gift. In the first place, culture was now made to include an openness to ideas, as well as fine manners and an appreciation of the beauty of fine poetry and fine prose. Indeed, of the two, the intellectual element is now the most prominent; the most powerful motive, according to Arnold, that prompts us to read the best books, to know the best that has been thought and said in the world, is now identified with the genuine scientific passion for "seeing things as they really are." But this is not all: Arnold will have us go deeper still and take a yet more comprehensive view. The passion for culture is not, he says, the mere desire of seeing things as they are, for the simple pleasure of seeing them as they are, and developing the intelligence of the seer; though this is a noble impulse, eminently proper to an intelligent being. But culture, true culture, aims at more than this: it aims at nothing less then human perfection, a perfect spiritual condition, involving the "harmonious expansion of all the powers which make the beauty and worth of human nature," and thus necessarily including perfection of will and of the moral feelings that claim the governance of will, no less than perfection of intelligence and taste. Its dominant idea being that of a human nature perfect on all its sides, it includes and transcends religion, which on its practical side is dominated by the more limited idea of moral perfection, and which, therefore, tends to concentrate effort on conquering the "obvious faults of our animality." So viewed, culture cannot be sought by anyone who seeks it for himself alone. "Because men are all members of one great whole, and the sympathy which is in human nature will not allow one member to have a perfect welfare independent of the rest, the expansion of our humanity, to suit the idea of perfection which culture forms, must be a *general* expansion. . . . The individual is obliged, under pain of being stunted and enfeebled in his own development if he disobeys, to carry others along with him in his march towards perfection, to be continually doing all he can to enlarge and increase the volume of the human stream sweeping thitherward." In this wider conception "all the love of our neighbour, the impulses towards action, help, and beneficence, the desire for clearing human confusion and diminishing the sum of human misery, the noble aspiration to leave the world better and happier than we found it"—all these motives "come in as part of the grounds of culture and the main and pre-eminent part." This culture is seen—if we see with Arnold's eyes—to move by the force not merely or primarily of the scientific impulse to pure knowledge, but also of the moral and social impulse to do good: it has "one great passion for sweetness and light"; and "one greater, for making reason and the will of God prevail."

Well, this was a noble ideal, and the words in which Arnold set it before us had the genuine ring of prophetic conviction; but we felt that we had travelled a long way from the Earl of Chesterfield and the admirable and consummate culture of the English aristocracy in the eighteenth century. Our historical reminiscences seemed to indicate that the passion for making reason and the will of God prevail, and carrying on the whole human race in a grand march towards complete spiritual perfection, which these fine gentlemen as a class derived from their studies in Greek and Latin, was of a very limited description; hardly, indeed, perceptible to the scrutiny of the impartial historian. Even in the latter half of the nineteenth century the desire to cultivate the intellect and taste by reading the best books, and the passion for social improvement, are not—if we look at actual facts—always found together; or even if we grant that the one can hardly exist without some degree of the other, at any rate they co-exist in different minds in very varying proportions. And when Arnold tells us that the Greeks had arrived, in theory at least, at a harmonious adjustment of the claims of both, we feel that his admiration for Hellenism has led him to idealize it; for we cannot but remember how Plato politely but firmly conducts the poets out of his republic, and how the Stoics sneered at Aristotle's praises of pure speculation. In short, we might allow Arnold to define the aim of culture either as the pursuit of sweetness and light, or more comprehensively as the pursuit of complete spiritual perfection, including the aim of making reason and the will of God prevail; but in the name of culture itself we must refuse to use the same word for two such different things; since the resulting confusion of thought will certainly impede our efforts to see things as they really are.

And when the alternatives are thus presented, it seems clear that usage is on the side of the narrower meaning. For what philanthropy is now increasingly eager to diffuse, under the name of culture, is something different from religion and morality; it is not these goods that have been withheld from the poor, nor of which the promotion excuses the luxurious expenditure of the rich. Poverty—except so far as it excludes even adequate moral instruction—is no bar to morality; as it is happily in men's power to do their duty in all relations of life, under any pressure of outward circumstances; and it is the rich, not the poor, that the Gospel warns of their special difficulty in entering the kingdom of heaven. Again if the pursuit of culture is taken to transcend and include the aim of promoting religion and morality, these sublimer goods cannot but claim the larger share of attention. Indeed Arnold himself told us in a later essay, that at least three-fourths of human life belong to morality, and religion as supplying motive force to morality; art and science together can at most claim the remaining fourth. But if so, in discussing the principles that should guide our effort after the improvement of the three-fourths of life that morality claims, the difficulties that such effort encounters, the methods which it has to apply, we shall inevitably find ourselves led far away from the consideration of culture in the ordinary sense.

For practical purposes then we must take the narrower meaning. But I have not referred to Arnold's wider notion in order merely to reject it, or to divorce the pursuit of culture from the larger aim at complete spiritual perfection and harmonious development of all sides of human nature. What god has joined together, I do not presume thus to put asunder. No one who has risen to the grand conception of the study of perfection as a comprehensive and balanced whole, the harmonious development of human nature on all its sides, can ever consent to abandon it; and therefore we cannot put it out of sight altogether, in considering the more restricted aims of culture in the narrower sense. This narrower notion is an abstraction needful for the purpose of clearer view and practical working out of methods of pursuit; but it should never be forgotten that the separation cannot be made complete without loss of truth. I propose, therefore, in what I have yet to say, first to analyse somewhat further the narrower conception of culture; and then to consider its relation to other elements of the wider notion of complete spiritual perfection.

The first question that arises when we concentrate attention on culture in the narrower and more usual sense is to determine its relation to knowledge. We certainly often distinguish the two: we speak of diffusing knowledge *and* culture; and yet it is not easy to conceive a cultivation of the mind that does not give knowledge. Here again it may help us to follow the course of Matthew Arnold's thought. In his earliest view, as we saw, culture seems to lie in the development of the taste rather than the intellect; the aristocracy, he finds, has culture but lacks ideas. But in his later and more meditated view he appears to blend the two completely, taking the development of the intellect as the more fundamental element. His favourite phrase for the essential spring of culture is the desire or passion for "seeing things as they are." The activity of culture, he tells us, lies in reading, observing, thinking. Hellenism—which is another term for culture in the narrower sense—"drives at ideas"; has "an ardent sense for all the new and changing combinations of them which man's activity brings with it, and an indomitable impulse to know and adjust them perfectly"; it drives at "an unclouded clearness" and flexibility of mind, an "unimpeded play of thought," an "untrammelled spontaneity of consciousness." This is its essential aim; and the sweetness, the grace and serenity, the sensibility to beauty, the aversion to hideousness, rawness, vulgarity, which Arnold no less values, are conceived to have an intellectual root and source; they are to come from "harmonized ideas."

Now, I agree generally with the view here expressed as to the primacy of the intellectual element of culture. Since the most essential function of the mind is to think and know, a man of cultivated mind must be essentially concerned for knowledge: but it is not knowledge merely that gives culture. A man may be learned and yet lack culture: for he may be a pedant, and the characteristic of a pedant is that he has knowledge without culture. So again, a load of facts retained in the memory, a mass of reasonings got up merely for examination, these are not, they do not give culture. It is the love of knowledge, the ardour of scientific curiosity, driving us continually to absorb new facts and ideas, to make them our own and fit them into the living and growing system of our thought; and the trained faculty of doing this, the alert and supple intelligence exercised and continually developed in doing this,—it is in these that culture essentially lies.

But when we consider how to acquire this habit of mind, we must, I think, regretfully take leave of the fascinating guide whom I have so long allowed to lead our thoughts on this subject. The path which at this point he shows us is a flowery one; but it does not climb the pass that we have to cross; it cannot bring us to the solution of our problem. For Matthew Arnold's method of seeking truth is a survival from a pre-scientific age. He is a man of letters pure and simple; and often seems quite serenely unconscious of the intellectual limitations of his type. How the crude matter of common experience is reduced to the order and system which constitutes it an object of scientific knowledge; how the precisest possible conceptions are applied in the exact apprehension and analysis of facts, and how by facts thus established and analysed the conceptions in their turn are gradually rectified; how the laws of nature are ascertained by the combined processes of induction and deduction, provisional assumption and careful verification; how a general hypothesis is used to guide inquiry, and after due comparison with ascertained particulars, becomes an accepted theory; and how a theory, receiving further confirmation, takes its place finally as an organic part of a vast, living, ever-growing system of knowledge;—all this is quite alien to the habitual thought of a mere man of letters. Yet it is this complex process that the desire to see things as they are must, in the present state of knowledge, prompt a man to learn, to follow, and to apply. Intellectual culture, at the end of the nineteenth century, must include as its most essential element a scientific habit of mind; and a scientific habit of mind can only be acquired by the methodical study of some part at least of what the human race has come scientifically to know.

Now of all this Arnold has a very faint and intermittent conception. His method of "seeing things as they are" is simply to read the best books of all ages and countries, and let the unimpeded play of his consciousness combine the results. We ought, he thinks, to read a good many books, to give our consciousness room to play in, and acquire the right flexibility of spirit; but we must especially read the books of great writers—such as those of whom he incidentally gives a list: Plato, Cicero, Machiavelli, Shakespeare, Voltaire, Goethe. Now imagine a man learning physical science in this way. I will take astronomy as the example most favourable to Arnold's view that I could choose; since students do still read the great work of Newton, though two centuries old: but imagine a learner, desirous of seeing the starry universe as it is, set down to read the treatises of Ptolemy, Copernicus, Galileo, Kepler, and let his consciousness play above them in an untrammelled manner, instead of learning astronomical theory from the latest books, and the actual method of astronomical observation in a modern observatory! And the suggestion would seem still more eccentric if applied to physics, chemistry, and biology.

It may be replied that, granting this true as to the knowledge of nature, the case is otherwise with knowledge of the human spirit. But the antithesis is misleading. Man, whatever else he is, is part of the world of nature, and modern science is more and more resolutely claiming him as an object of investigation. The sciences that deal with man viewed on his spiritual side—psychology and sociology—are certainly in a rudimentary condition compared with the physical sciences, and have fundamental difficulties to overcome of a kind no longer found in those more established methods. But literature supplies no short cut for overcoming these difficulties: the intuitions of literary genius will not avail to reduce to scientific order the complicated facts of psychical experience, any more than the facts of the physical world. And this is no less true of those special branches of the study of social man, which have attained a more advanced condition than the general science of society that, in idea, comprehends them:—economics, political science, archæology, philology. Let us take philology, because, being concerned about words, it is in a way akin to literature. Reflection at once shows that the kinship lies entirely in the object and not at all in the manner of study. This is true even of the most limited species of philology, the study of the grammar of a particular language. The *Iliad* read by a man of letters differs in aspect from the *Iliad* scrutinized by the student of Greek philology, much as the Niagara of the ordinary cultivated tourist differs from Niagara as observed by the student of hydrodynamics. In short, in dealing with the human spirit and its products, no less than with merely physical phenomena, we shall find that "letting our consciousness play about a subject" is an essentially different thing from setting our intellect at work upon it methodically: and it is the latter habit that has to be resolutely learnt by any modern mind, that is earnestly desirous of "seeing things as they are."

And when this is clearly apprehended, it becomes manifest that the aim of science, and the aspect which things scientifically known present to the mind, is profoundly different from the aim of art, and the aspect of things which the study of beauty aims at seizing and presenting. There is, indeed, at the same time, a deep affinity traceable between the two. Things seen as they are by science afford the seer the pleasure of complex harmony, through the unity of intelligible order and system that is seen to pervade the vast diversity of particular facts, when we are able to bring them under general laws: and the pleasure of harmony, of a subtle unity of effect pervading a diversity of sensible impressions, is a main element of the delight derived from a great work of art. But the harmony and its elements are essentially different in the two cases; and in the case of science the harmony is essentially known, intellectually grasped, the feeling of it secondary; whereas in the case of art the feeling is of primary importance, the intellectual explanation of it secondary. So again the *technique* of art always involves knowledge of some kinds, and in the representative arts especially, careful observation of facts: but the knowledge is not sought for its own sake, and there is no general need that the facts should be scientifically understood. It would seem therefore that these two elements of what we commonly call culture, the love of truth along with the trained faculty for attaining it, and the love of beauty duly trained and developed, are—speaking broadly—as different in their aims and points of view as either is different from morality.

At this point Arnold would answer—this answer is, in fact, his final utterance on the subject—that it is the special function of literature to comprehend and mediate between these divergent aims and views. He urges that what the spirit of man—even the most modern man—demands is to establish a satisfactory relation between the results of science and our sense of conduct and sense of beauty; and that this is what humane letters, poetry and eloquence, stirring our higher emotions, will do for us. In this answer there is an important element of truth; but the claim goes too far. For to satisfy completely the demand to which he appeals, to bring into true and clear intellectual relation the notions and methods of studies so diverse as positive science and the theory of the fine arts is more than literature as literature can perform; the result can only be attained by philosophy, whose peculiar task indeed it is to bring into clear, orderly, harmonious relations the fundamental notions and methods of all special sciences and studies. But we must admit that it is not a task which philosophy can yet be said to have triumphantly accomplished: the height from which all normal human aims and activities can be clearly and fully contemplated in true and harmonious relations is a height not yet surmounted by the human spirit. And perhaps it never will be surmounted; perhaps—to change the metaphor—the accomplishment of this task is an ideal whose face is

> *Evermore unseen,*
> *And fixed upon the far sea-line,*

which changes with every advance in the endless voyaging of the human spirit.

In the meantime it may be conceded to the advocates of humane letters that literature of the thoughtful kind—such poetry and eloquence as really deserves to be called a criticism of life—may supply even to philosophers an important part of the matter of philosophy, though it cannot give philosophic form and order, and may give a provisional substitute for philosophy to the many who do not philosophize. It gives, or helps to give, the kind of wide interest in, the versatile sympathy with, the whole complex manifestation of the human spirit in human history, which is required as a corrective to the specialization that the growth of science inexorably imposes; and giving this along with beauty and distinction of form and expression, it does at any rate bridge the gulf we occasionally feel between the divergent aims of science and art. It helps to produce a harmony of feeling in our contemplation of the world and life presented under these diverse aspects; if not the reasoned harmony of ideas which only philosophy could impart. And it is this function of literature, I think, that affords the best justification for the prominence given to it in our educational system.

So far, in analysing the conception of culture in the narrower sense, we have found divergence, at first sight wide, between the two elements of it which we have distinguished, but we have not found discord. Can we say that this is still the case when we turn to consider culture in relation to other elements of the wider notion of spiritual perfection? Is there any natural opposition between the devotion to moral excellence and the devotion to knowledge or to beauty? and if so, how are we to deal with it? These are questions of some practical importance on which it remains to say a few words.

First, as regards science and the scientific habit of mind. Here we may say broadly that morality is disposed to welcome science as a *servant,* but somewhat to dread it as a *master.* No moralist would deny that we shall be better able to promote human well-being or cure human woes the more we can learn from science of the conditions of both: discord can only arise because science is not altogether willing to accept simply this subordinate and serviceable relation to ethics. I shall not here treat of the deepest element of this discord: the tendency of the scientific study of man, in explaining the origin and growth of moral ideas and sentiments, to explain away their binding force; so that the "law so analysed" ceases, as Browning says, to "coerce you much." This is a difficulty with which only a systematic moral philosophy can deal. But, assuming that all such presumptuous invasions of science are repelled, and ethics allowed to be valid within its own domain, the question still remains how far the study of science tends to produce a habit of mind unfavourable to moral ardour. I think some such effect must be allowed to be natural. Scientific curiosity naturally adopts a neutral attitude towards the evil and good in the world it seeks to know; it aims at understanding, explaining, tracing the causes of the former no less than the latter; and so far as cases of vice and wrongdoing present interesting problems to science, the solution of which throws light on psychological and sociological laws, the passion for discovering truth seems inevitably to carry with it a certain pleasure in the existence of the facts scientifically understood and explained, which is difficult to reconcile with the aversion to vice and wrongdoing that morality would inculcate.

We may illustrate this by comparing the similar attitude towards physical evil sometimes noticed in students of medical science. We have all heard of the surgeon who, when bicycles came in, rubbed his hands with delight over the novel and beautiful fractures of the lower limbs resulting from this mode of progression! But though the surgeon's sentiments towards an interesting fracture are different from a layman's, and may have an intermingling of scientific satisfaction from which the latter recoils, we all know that this does not normally affect his active impulses; in the presence of the need of action he is none the less helpful, while the layman is comparatively helpless. And perhaps the parallel may suggest a tolerable practical solution of the deeper discord between the scientific and the moral views of man's mental nature. That is, though there must perhaps be some interference in the region of *feeling* between the passion of scientific activity and normal ethical sentiment, there need be none in respect of habits of *action*. And any loss in the region of sentiment will not be uncompensated; for the keener and correcter insight into the bad consequences of our actions which science may be expected to give, must tend to direct the sentiment of moral aversion to matters other than those on which ordinary morality concentrates its attention, and thus to make its scope at once broader and truer.

When we turn to contemplate the pursuit of beauty in relation to the pursuit of moral excellence we find an occasional antagonism even more sharply marked, just because of the affinity between the two. Morality and Art sometimes appear as the proverbial "two of a trade" that cannot agree;—and in speaking of art I mean only work worthy of the name, and do not include the mere misuse of technical gifts for the gratification of base appetites. Both art and morality have an ideal, and the aim in both cases is to apprehend and exhibit the ideal in a reality that does not conform to or express it adequately; but the ideals are not the same, and it is just where they most nearly coincide—in dealing with human life and character—that some conflict is apt to arise. Morality aims at eradicating and abolishing evil, especially moral evil; whereas the æsthetic contemplation of life recognizes it as an element necessary to vivid and full interest. The opposition attains its sharpest edge in modern realistic art and literature; but it is by no means confined to the work of this school. Take, for example, the *Paradise Lost* of Milton—a writer as unlike a modern realist as possible. The old remark, that Satan is the real hero of *Paradise Lost*, is an epigrammatic exaggeration; but he is certainly quite indispensable to the interest of the poem; and the magnificent inconsistency with which Milton has half humanized his devil shows that he felt this. If the description of Adam and Eve in the Miltonian Paradise is not dull—and most of us, I think, do not find it dull—it is because we know that the devil is on his way thither; the charm of the placid, innocent life requires to be flavoured by the anticipated contrast. Thus, æsthetically speaking, the more we admire the poem the more satisfaction we must find in the existence of the devil, as an indispensable element of the whole artistic construction; and this satisfaction is liable to clash somewhat with our moral attitude towards evil.

I do not think that this opposition can be altogether overcome. Its root lies deep in the nature of things as we are compelled to conceive it; it represents an unsolved problem of philosophy, which continually forces itself to the front in the development of the religious consciousness. The general man is convinced that the war with moral evil is essential to that highest human life which is the highest thing we know in the world of experience; and yet he is no less convinced that the world with all its evil is somehow good, as the outcome and manifestation of ideal goodness. The aim of art and of the effort to apprehend beauty corresponds to the latter of these convictions; and thus its claim to have a place along with moral effort, in our ideal of human nature harmoniously developed, is strongly based. If so, it would seem that we must endeavour to make the moods of æethetic and ethical sentiment alternate, if we cannot quite harmonize them; the delighted contemplation of our mingled and varied world as beautiful in its mixtures and contrasts, though it cannot be allowed to interfere with the moral struggle with evil, may be allowed to relieve it, and give a transient repose from conflict.

And on the whole we must be content that science and art and morality are for the most part working on the same side, in that struggle with our lower nature through which we "move upward, working out the beast." Perhaps they will aid each other best if we abstain from trying to drill them into perfect conformity of movement, and allow them to fight independently in loose array.

IX

UNREASONABLE ACTION

IN the present paper I wish to examine the conception of what I think it on the whole most convenient to call the "unreasonable action" of sane persons in an apparently normal condition; and to contribute, if possible, to the more precise ascertainment of the nature of the mental process involved in it. The subject is one which attracted considerable attention in Greek philosophy; since the cardinal doctrine of Socrates "that every man wishes for his own good and would get it if he knew how" naturally brought into prominence the question, "How then is it that men continually choose to do what they apparently know will not conduce to their own good?" Accordingly the Aristotelian treatment of ethics* included an elaborate discussion of the "want of self-restraint" exhibited in such acts, considered primarily in the special case of indulgence of bodily appetites in spite of a conviction that they ought not be be indulged. The discussion, apart from its historical interest, may still be read with profit; but the

This essay was printed in *Mind* (vol. ii., N.S. No. 6).
*I refer to book VII of the *Nicomachean Ethics.*

combination of "dialectical" and "naturalistic" methods which the writer uses is somewhat confusing to a modern reader; and the *node* of the difficulty with which he deals seems to me to be rather evaded than overcome. In modern psychological and ethical treatises the question has, from various causes, usually failed to receive the full and systematic treatment, which it appears to me to deserve; and this is the main reason why I wish now to draw attention to it.

I must begin by defining more clearly the phenomenon that I have in view. In the first place, I wish to include inaction as well as positive action—the not doing what we judge that we ought to do, no less than the doing what we judge that we ought not to do. Secondly, I mean action not *objectively* but *subjectively* unreasonable; i.e., not action which is contrary to *sound* judgment, but action which is done in conscious opposition to the practical judgment of the agent at the time. Such practical judgment will in many cases be the result of a process of reasoning of some kind, either performed immediately before the act is done or at some previous time; in these cases the term "unreasonable" seems obviously appropriate. I shall, however, extend the term to cases in which the judgment opposed to the act is apparently intuitive, and not inferential. The propriety of this extension might, I admit, be questioned: but I want a term to cover both the cases above distinguished, and I can find no other familiar term so convenient. I wish then to examine consciously unreasonable action, in this sense, as a fact of experience capable of being observed and analysed, without reference to the validity of the judgment involved in it, or of the process (if any) of reasoning by which it has been reached; simply with the view of finding out, by reflective observation, exactly what it is that happens when one knowingly acts against one's "better judgment."

Again, by "practical judgment" I do not necessarily mean what is ordinarily called "moral judgment" or "dictate of conscience," or of the "moral faculty." I mean, of course, to include this as one species of the phenomenon to be discussed; but in my view, and, I think, in the view of Commonsense, there are many cases of consciously unreasonable action where morality in the ordinary sense does not supply the judgment to which the act is opposed. Let us suppose that a man regards ordinary social morality as a mere external code sanctioned by public opinion, which the adequately instructed and emancipated individual only obeys so far as he conceives it to be on the whole his interest to do so: still, as Butler pointed out, the conflict between Reason and Unreason remains in the experience of such a man in the form of a conflict of passion and appetite with what he judges from time to time to be conducive to his interest on the whole.

But if the notion of subjectively unreasonable action is thus, from one point of view, wider than that of subjectively wrong action, it would seem to be from another point of view narrower. For action subjectively wrong would be widely held to include action which conflicts with the agent's moral *sentiment,* no less than action which is contrary to his practical *judgment;*—moral sentiment being conceived as a species of emotion not necessarily connected with a judgment as to what "ought to be done" by the agent or what is "good" for him. Indeed, in the account of the moral consciousness that some writers of repute give, the emotional element is alone explicitly recognized: the moral consciousness appears to be conceived merely as a species of complex emotion mixed of baser and nobler elements—the baser element being the vague associations of pain with wrong acts, due to experiences of the disagreeable effects of retaliation, punishment, and loss of social reputation, and associations of pleasure with acts that win praise, goodwill and reciprocal services from other men; the nobler being sympathy with the painful consequences to others of bad acts, and the pleasurable consequences of good acts.

This is not my view: I regard it as an essential characteristic of moral sentiment that it involves a judgment, either explicit or implicit, that the act to which the sentiment is directed "ought" or "ought not" to be done. But I do not wish here to enter into any controversy on this point: I merely desire now to point out that conduct may be opposed to moral sentiment, according to the view of moral sentiment above given, without having the characteristic of subjective unreasonableness; and, again, this characteristic may belong to conduct in harmony with what would be widely regarded as moral sentiment. Suppose (e.g.) a religious persecutor yielding to a humane sentiment and remitting torture from a weak impulse of sympathy with a heretic, contrary to his conviction as to his religious duty; or suppose Machiavelli's prince yielding to a social impulse and impairing his hold on power from a weak reluctance to kill an innocent person, contrary to his conviction as to what is conducive to his interest on the whole. In either case the persecutor or the tyrant would act contrary to his deliberate judgment as to what it would be best for him to do, and therefore with 'subjective unreasonableness'; but in both cases the sentiment that prompted his action would seem to be properly classed as a moral sentiment, according to the view above described. And in the latter case he certainly would not be commonly judged to act wrongly,—even according to a subjective standard of wrongness;—while in the former case it is at least doubtful whether he would be so judged.

By "unreasonable action," then, I mean voluntary action contrary to a man's deliberate judgment as to what is right or best for him to do: such judgment being at least implicitly present when the action is willed. I therefore exclude what may be called "purely impulsive" acts: i.e., acts which so rapidly and immediately follow some powerful impulse of desire, anger, or fear, that there is no room for any judgment at all as to their rightness or wrongness: not only is there no clear and explicit judgment with which the will conflicts, but not even a symbol or suggestion of such a judgment. But often when there is no explicit judgment there is an uneasy feeling which a pause for reflection might develop into a judgment: and sometimes when we recall such states of mind there is a difficulty in saying whether this uneasy feeling did or did not contain an implicit judgment that the act was wrong. For it often happens that uneasy feelings similar to ordinary moral sentiments—I have elsewhere called them "quasi-moral"—accompany voluntary acts done strictly in accordance with the agent's practical judgment; i.e., when such acts are opposed to widely accepted rules of conduct, or include among their foreseen consequences annoyance to other human beings. Hence in trying to observe and analyse my own experiences of unreasonable action I have found a difficulty in dealing with cases in which a moral (or prudential) judgment, if present at all, was only implicitly present: since when subsequent reflection shows a past deed to have been clearly contrary to one's normal judgment as to what is right or best, this subsequent conviction is apt to mix itself with one's memory of the particular state of mind in which the deed was actually done. In this way what was really a quite vague feeling of uneasiness may be converted in memory into a more definite symbol of a judgment opposed to the volition that actually took place. I have tried, however, to be on my guard against this source of error in the observations which have led me to the conclusions that I am about to state.

Finally, I must define somewhat further the limitation of my subject to the experience of persons apparently sane, and in an apparently normal condition. I mean by this to exclude from discussion all cases of discord between voluntary act and rational judgment, when the agent's will is manifestly in an abnormal condition,—either from some distinct cerebral disease, or from some transient disturbance of his normal mental condition due to drugs, extreme heat, sudden calamity, or any other physical or psychical cause. Cases of this kind—in which there appears to be no loss of sanity, in the ordinary sense, the mental disturbance affecting the will and not the reason—are highly interesting from a psychological point of view, as well as from that of medicine or jurisprudence. Sometimes they are cases of "aboulia" or impotence of will, when in spite of perfect clearness in a man's practical judgment he feels it simply impossible to form an effective volition in accordance with his judgment; sometimes, again, to use M. Ribot's* terms, he suffers from "excess" and not "defect" of "impulsion," and appears to himself compelled to commit some atrocious crime or grotesque folly, or otherwise to act in a manner contrary to his practical judgment, under the constraint of an impulse which he feels to be irresistible. But in either case the very characteristics that give these phenomena their striking interest render it desirable to reserve them for separate discussion.

The line between "normality" and "abnormality" cannot, indeed, be precisely drawn; and certain phenomena, similar in kind to those just mentioned, though much slighter in degree, fall within the experience of ordinarily sane persons free from any perceptible organic disorder or disturbance. I can myself recall momentary impressions of something like "aboulia"; i.e., moments in which I was transiently conscious of an apparent impossibility of willing to do something which I judged it right to do, and which appeared to be completely within the control of my will. And though I have not myself had any similar experience of irresistible "excess of impulsion," I see no reason to doubt that others have had such experiences, apart from any recongnizable cerebral disorder; it would seem that hunger and thirst, aversion to death or to extreme pain, the longing for alcohol, opium, etc., occasionally reach a point of intensity at which they are felt as irresistibly overpowering rational choice. But cases of either kind are at any rate very exceptional in the experience of

---

* See *Les Maladies de la Volonté,* par Th. Ribot.

ordinary men; and I propose to exclude them from consideration at present, no less than the more distinct "maladies de la volonté" before mentioned. I wish to concentrate attention on the ordinary experiences of "yielding to temptation," where this consciousness of the impossibility of resistance does not enter in; where, however strong may be the rush of anger or appetite that comes over a man, it certainly does not present itself as invincible. This purely subjective distinction seems to afford a boundary line *within* which it is not difficult to keep, though it would doubtless be difficult or impossible to draw it exactly.

It may tend to clearness to define the experiences that I wish to examine as those in which there is an *appearance* of free choice of the unreasonable act by the agent,—however this appearance may be explained away or shown to be an illusion. At the same time I do not at all wish to mix up the present discussion with a discussion on Free Will. The connection of "subjective irrationality"—or, at least, "subjective wrongness"—and "freedom" is, indeed, obvious and natural from a jural point of view,—so far at least as the popular view of punishment as retributive and the popular conceptions of Desert and Imputation are retained: since in this view it would seem that "subjective wrongness" must go along with "freedom" in order to constitute an act fully deserving of punishment. For the jurist's maxim "Ignorantia juris non excusat" is not satisfactory to the plain man's sense of equity: to punish any one for doing what he at the time did not know to be wrong appears to the plain man at best a regrettable exercise of society's right of self-preservation, and not a realization of ideal justice. But in a psychological inquiry there seems to me no ground whatever for mixing up the question whether acts are, metaphysically speaking, "free" with the question whether they are accompanied with a consciousness of their irrationality.

I incline, however, to think that the tendency to fuse the two questions, and the prominence in the fusion of the question of Free Will, partly explain the fact that the very existence of unreasonable action appears to be not sufficiently recognized by influential writers of the most opposite schools of philosophy.

I find that such writers are apt to give an account of voluntary action which—without expressly denying the existence of what I call subjective irrationality—appears to leave no room for it. They admit, of course, that there are abundant instances of acts condemned, as contrary to sound practical principles, not only by the judgment of other men but by the subsequent judgment of the agent; but in the analysis which they give of the state of mind in which such actions are willed, they appear to place the source of error in the intellect alone and not at all in the relation of the will to the intellect. For instance, Bentham affirms that "on the occasion of every act he exercises, every human being is led to pursue that line of conduct which, according to his view of the case, taken by him at the moment, will be in the highest degree contributory to his own greatest happiness";* and as Bentham also holds that the "constantly proper end of action on the part of every individual at the moment of action is his real greatest happiness from that moment to the end of his life,"† there would seem to be no room for what I call "subjective unreasonableness." If Bentham's doctrine is valid, the defect of a volition which actually results in a diminution of the agent's happiness must always lie in the man's "view of the case taken at the moment": the evils which reflection would show to be overwhelmingly probable consequences of his act, manifestly outweighing any probable good to result from it, are not present to his mind in the moment of willing; or if they are in some degree present, they are, at any rate, not correctly represented in imagination or thought. The only way therefore of improving his outward conduct must be to correct his tendencies to err by defect or excess in the intellectual representation of future consequences: as he always acts in accordance with his judgment as to what is most likely to conduce to his greatest happiness, if only all errors of judgment were corrected, he would always act for his real greatest happiness. (I may add that so acting, in Bentham's view, he would also always act in the way most conducive to general happiness: but with the question of the harmony of interests in human society we are not now concerned.)

I do not think that Bentham's doctrine on this point was accepted in its full breadth by his more influential disciples. Certainly J. S. Mill appears to admit important exceptions to it, both in the direction of self-sacrifice and in the direction of self-indulgence. He admits, on the one hand, that the "hero or the martyr" often has "voluntarily" to "do without happiness" for the sake of "something which he prizes more than his own

---

* Bentham, *Constitutional Code,* Introduction, p. 2 (vol. ix. of Bowning's edition).
† Bentham, *Memoirs,* p. 560 (vol. x. of Bowning's edition).

individual happiness"; and he admits, on the other hand, that "men often from infirmity of character, make their election for the nearer good, though they know it to be the less valuable; and this no less when the choice is between two bodily pleasures, than when it is between bodily and mental. They pursue sensual indulgence to the injury of health, though perfectly aware that health is the greater good."[*] But though Mill gives a careful psychological analysis[†] of the former deviation from the pursuit of apparent self-interest, he does not pay the same attention to the latter; and yet it is difficult to reconcile the conscious self-sacrifice—if I may be allowed the term—of the voluptuary, no less than the conscious self-sacrifice of the moral hero, with Mill's general view that "to desire anything, except in proportion as the idea of it is pleasant, is a physical impossibility." For in balancing "sensual indulgences" against "injury to health," distinctions of quality hardly come in; the prudential estimate, in which the pleasure of champagne at dinner is seen to be outweighed by the headache next morning, is surely quantitative rather than qualitative: hence when the voluptuary chooses a "pleasure known to be the less valuable" it would seem that he must choose something of which—in a certain sense—the "idea" is less "pleasant" than the idea of the consequences that he rejects. If so, some explanation of this imprudent choice seems to be required; and in order to give it, we have to examine more closely the nature of the mental phenomenon in which what he calls "infirmity of character" in manifested.

But before I proceed to this examination, I wish to point out that the tendency either to exclude the notion of "wilful unreasonableness," or to neglect to examine the fact which it represents, is not found only in psychologists of Bentham's school; who regard pleasure and the avoidance of pain as the sole normal motives of human action, and the attainment of the greatest balance of pleasure over pain—to self or to other sentient beings—as the only "right and proper" end of such action. We find this tendency also in writers who sweepingly reject and controvert the Hedonism of Bentham and Mill. For example, in Green's *Prolegomena to Ethics*, both the psychological doctrine that pleasure is the normal motive of human action, and the ethical doctrine that it is the proper motive, are

---

[*] *Utilitarianism*, chap. ii.
[†] *Ibid.*, chap. iv.

controverted with almost tedious emphasis and iteration. But Green still lays down as broadly as Bentham that every person in every moral action, virtuous or vicious, presents to himself some possible state or achievement of his own as for the time his greatest good, and acts for the sake of that good; at the same time explaining that the kind of good which a person at any point of his life "presents to himself as greatest depends on his past experience."* From these and other passages we should certainly infer that, in Green's view, vicious choice is always made in the illusory belief that the act chosen is conducive to the agent's greatest good; although Green is on this point less clearly consistent than Bentham, since he also says that "the objects where good is actually sought are often not those where reason, even as in the person seeking them, pronounces that it is to be found."† But passages in the former sense are more common in his book, and he seems to make no attempt to bring them into harmony with that last quoted.

I cannot accept the proposition "that every man always acts for the sake of what he presents to himself as his own greatest good," whether it is offered in a hedonistic or in a non-hedonistic form. At the same time, I think that the statements which I have quoted from Bentham and Green are by no means to be treated as isolated paradoxes of individual thinkers; I think they point to a difficulty widely felt by educated persons, in accepting and applying the notion of "wilful wrongdoing," i.e., conscious choice of alternatives of action known to be in conflict with principles still consciously accepted by the agent. On the other hand, this notion of wilful wrongdoing is so clearly a part of the common moral experience of mankind that it seems very paradoxical to reject it, or explain it away.

Under these circumstances it seemed to me worth while to make a systematic attempt to observe with as much care as possible—and as soon as possible after the phenomenon had occurred—the mental process that actually takes place in the case of unreasonable action. I have found some difficulty in making the observations; because action consciously unreasonable belongs to the class of phenomena which tend to be prevented by attempts to direct attention to them. This result is not, indeed, to be deprecated from a practical point of view; indeed, it may, I think, be fairly

---

* Green, *Prolegomena to Ethics,* book ii., chap. i., f. 99.
† *l.c.,* book iii., chap. i., f. 177.

urged as a practical argument for the empirical study of the present psychological problem, not only that the results of systematic self-observation directed to this point are likely to aid the observer in his moral efforts to avoid acting unreasonably, but that the mere habitual direction of his attention to this problem tends to diminish his tendency to consciously unreasonable conduct. But though practically advantageous, this latter result is, from a scientific point of view, inconvenient. This direction of attention, however, cannot be long maintained; and in the intervals in which it is otherwise directed the psychological observer is probably as liable to act unreasonably as any one else; though probably the phenomenon does not last quite as long in his case, since, as soon as he is clearly conscious of so acting, the desire to observe the process is likely to be developed and to interfere with the desire which is stimulating the unreasonable volition.

I also recognize that I ought not to put forward confidently the results that follow as typical and fairly representative of the experiences of men in general. It is a generally recognized obstacle in the way of psychological study, especially in the region of the intellect and the emotions, that the attitude of introspective observation must be supposed to modify to some extent the phenomena observed; while at the same time it is difficult to ascertain and allow for the amount of effect thus produced. Now in relation to the experiences with which I am here concerned, the attitude of disengaged observant attention is peculiarly novel and unfamiliar, and therefore its distrubing effect may reasonably be supposed to be peculiarly great. I have, accordingly, endeavoured as far as possible to check the conclusions that I should draw from my own experience by observation and interpretation of the words and conduct of others. My conclusion on the whole would be that—in the case of reflective persons—a *clear* consciousness that an act is what ought not to be done, accompanying a voluntary determination to do it, is a comparatively rare phenomenon. It is, indeed, a phenomenon that does occur, and I will presently examine it more closely: but first it will be convenient to distinguish from it several other states of mind in which acts contrary to general resolutions deliberately adopted by the agent may be done; as most of these are, in my experience, decidedly more common than unreasonable action with a clear consciousness of its unreasonableness. These other states of mind fall under two heads: (1) cases in which there is at the time no consciousness at all of a conflict between volition and practical judgment; and (2) cases in which such consciousness is present but only obscurely present.

Under the former head we may distinguish first the case of what are commonly called thoughtless or impulsive acts. I do not now mean the sudden "purely impulsive" acts of which I spoke before: but acts violating an accepted general rule, which, though they have been preceded by a certain amount of consideration and comparison, have been willed in a state of mind entirely devoid of any application of the general rule infringed to the particular case. Suppose, for instance, that a man has received a provocative letter in relation to some important business in which he is engaged: he will sometimes answer it in angry haste, although he has previously adopted a general resolution to exclude the influence of angry feeling in a correspondence of this kind by interposing an interval of time, sufficient ordinarily to allow his heated emotion to subside. I conceive that often, at least, in such cases the rule is simply forgotten for a time, just as a matter of fact might be: the effect of emotion is simply to exclude it temporarily from the man's memory.

I notice, however, that in the Aristotelian treatise before mentioned an alternative possibility is suggested, which may sometimes be realized in the case of impulsive acts. It is suggested that the general rule—say 'that letters should not be written in anger'—may be still present to the mind; though the particular judgment, 'My present state of mind is a state of anger'—required as a minor premiss for a practical syllogism leading to the right conclusion—is not made. And no doubt it may happen that an angry man is quite unaware that he is angry; in which case this minor premiss may be at the time absent through pure ignorance. But more often he is at least obscurely conscious of his anger; and if he is conscious of it at all, and has the general rule in his mind, it seems to me hardly possible that he should not be at least obscurely aware that the particular case comes under the rule.

More commonly, I think, when a general resolution is remembered, while yet the particular conclusion which ought to be drawn is not drawn, the cause of the phenomenon is a temporary perversion of judgment by some seductive feeling—such as anger, appetite, vanity, laziness. In such cases a man may either consciously suspend his general rule from a temporary conviction caused by the seductive feeling that he has adopted it without sufficient reason, or he may erroneously but sincerely persuade himself that it is not applicable to the case before him. Suppose he is at dinner and the champagne comes round: he is a patient of Sir Andrew Clark,★ and has already drunk the very limited amount allowed per month by that rigid adviser; but rapidly the arguments of Dr. Mortimer Granville occur to his mind, and he momentarily but sincerely becomes persuaded that though an extra glass may cause him a little temporary inconvenience, it will in the long run conduce to the maintenance of his physical tone. Or, as before, he has received a letter that rouses his indignation: he remembers his rule against allowing temper to influence his answer; but momentarily—under the influence of heated feeling—arrives at a sincere conviction that this rule of prudence ought to give way to his duty to society, which clearly requires him not to let so outrageous a breach of propriety go unreproved. Or having sat down to a hard and distasteful task which he regards it as his duty to do—but which can be postponed without any immediate disagreeable consequences to himself—he finds a difficulty in getting under way; and then rapidly but sincerely persuades himself that in the present state of his brain some lighter work is just at present more suited to his powers,—such as the study, through the medium of the daily papers, of current political events, of which no citizen ought to allow himself to be ignorant.

I have taken trivial illustrations because, being not complicated by ethical doubts and disagreements, they exemplify the phenomenon in question most clearly and simply. But I think that in graver cases a man is sometimes sincerely though very temporarily convinced by the same kind of fallacious reasoning—under the influence of some seductive feeling—that a general resolution previously made *either* ought to be abrogated or suspended *or* is inapplicable to the present case. Such a man will afterwards see the fallacy of the reasoning: but he may not have been even obscurely conscious at the time that it was fallacious.

But, again, these examples will also serve as illustrations of a different and, I think, still more common class of cases which fall under my second head; in which the man who yields to the fallacious process of reasoning

---

★ I have left unaltered the name of this eminent physician, who was alive when the article was written; since there is no other name that would, at that time, have seemed equally appropriate.

is dimly aware that it is fallacious. That is, shortly, the man sophisticates himself, being obscurely conscious of the sophistry.

Moralists have often called attention to sophistry of this kind, but I think they have not fully recognized how common it is, or done justice to its persistent, varied, and versatile ingenuity.

If the judgment which Desire finds in its way is opposed to the common-sense of mankind, as manifested in their common practice, the deliberating mind will impress on itself the presumption of differing from a majority so large: if, on the other hand, the restraining dictate of reason is one generally accepted, the fallibility of common-sense, and the importance of the individual's independence, will be placed in a strong light. If a novel indulgence is desired, the value of personal experience before finally deciding against it will be persuasively presented; if the longing is for an old familiar gratification, experience will seem to have shown that it may be enjoyed with comparative impunity. If the deliberating mind is instructed in ethical controversy, the various sceptical topics that may be culled from the mutual criticisms of moralists will offer almost inexhaustible resources of self-sophistication—such as the illusoriness of intuition, if the judgment is intuitive; if it is a reasoned conclusion, the fact that so many thoughtful persons reject the assumptions on which the reasoning is based. The Determinist will eagerly recognize the futility of now resisting the formed tendencies of his nature; the Libertarian will contemplate his indefeasible power of resisting them next time. The fallacies vary indefinitely; if plausible arguments are not available, absurd ones will often suffice: by hook or by crook, a quasi-rational conclusion on the side of desire will be attained.

Often, however, the seductive influence of feeling is of a more subtle kind than in the instances above given, and operates not by producing positively fallacious reasoning, but by directing attention *to* certain aspects of the subject, and *from* certain others. This (e.g.) is, I think, not uncommonly the case when an ordinarily well-bred and well-meaning man acts unreasonably from egotism or vanity: he has an obscure well-founded consciousness that he might come to a different view of his position if he resolutely faced certain aspects of it tending to reduce his personal claims; but he consciously refrains from directing attention to them. So, again, in cases where prompt action is necessary, passion may cause a man to acquiesce in acting on a one-sided view, while yet obscurely aware that the need is not so urgent as really to allow no time for adequate consideration.

In both the classes of cases last mentioned we may say that the wrongdoing is really wilful though not clearly so: the man is obscurely conscious either that the intellectual process leading him to a conclusion opposed to a previous resolution is unsound, or that he *might* take into account considerations which he *does* not distinctly contemplate and that he ought to take them into account. But though he is obscurely conscious of this, the sophistical or one-sided reasoning which leads him to the desired practical conclusion is more clearly present.

Finally, there remains pure undisguised wilfulness—where a man with his eyes open simply refuses to act in accordance with his practical judgment, although the latter is clearly present in his consciousness, and his attention is fully directed towards it. I think it undeniable that this phenomenon occurs: but my experience would lead me to conclude that—at least in the case of habitually reflective persons—it more often takes place in the case of negative action, non-performance of known duty: in the case of positive wrong action some process by which the opposing judgment is somehow thrust into the background of consciousness seems to me normally necessary. In other words, it seems, so far as this experience goes, to be far easier for a desire clearly recognized as conflicting with reason to inhibit action than to cause it.

Even in the exceptional case of a man openly avowing that he is acting contrary to what he knows to be both his interest and his duty, it cannot be assumed that a clear conviction of the truth of what he is saying is necessarily present to his consciousness. For a man's words in such a case may express not a present conviction, but the mere memory of a past conviction; moreover, one of the forms in which the ingenuity of self-sophistication is shown is the process of persuading oneself that a brave and manly self-identification with a vicious desire is better than a weak, self-deceptive submission to it;—or even than a feeble fluctuation between virtue and vice. Thus, even a man who said, "Evil, be thou my good," and acted accordingly, might have only an obscured consciousness of the awful irrationality of his action—obscured by a fallacious imagination that his only chance of being in any way admirable, at the point which he has now reached in his downward course, must lie in candid and consistent wickedness.